RICH SHEPHERD

POOR SHEEP

*The Call
To Accountability*

CARLOS L. MALONE, SR.

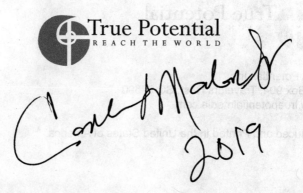

Copyright © 2018 Carlos L. Malone, Sr.

All rights reserved.

No part of this publication may be reproduced, stored, or transmitted in any form or by any means, including written, copied, or electronically, without prior written permission from the author or her agents. The only exception is brief quotations in printed reviews. Short excerpts may be used with the expressed written permission of the publisher or author.

Rich Shepherd, Poor Sheep
The Call To Accountability

Cover design by Carlos Malone, Jr.
Interior page design by True Potential, Inc.

ISBN: 978-1-948794-30-5 (paperback)
ISBN: 978-1-948794-31-2 (ebook)

True Potential, Inc.
PO Box 904, Travelers Rest, SC 29690
www.truepotentialmedia.com

Produced and Printed in the United States of America.

The Rich Shepherd, Poor Sheep Prayer

Give your love of justice to the king, O God, and righteousness to the king's son. Help him judge your people in the right way; let the poor always be treated fairly. May the mountains yield prosperity for all, and may the hills be fruitful. Help him to defend the poor, to rescue the children of the needy, and to crush their oppressors. May they fear you as long as the sun shines, as long as the moon remains in the sky. Yes, forever! May the king's rule be refreshing like spring rain on freshly cut grass, like the showers that water the earth. May all the godly flourish during his reign. May there be abundant prosperity until the moon is no more. — Psalm 72:1–7, NLT

Contents

The Rich Shepherd, Poor Sheep Prayer.........................3
Prologue.........................7
Acknowledgments.........................9
Introduction.........................12

Chapter One
The Call Versus Compromise.........................15

Chapter Two
Whose Sheep Are They Anyway?.........................20

Chapter Three
Lead Them, Feed Them, But Don't Need Them.........................33

Chapter Four
Because You Can, Should You?.........................47

Chapter Five
When Is Enough, Enough?.........................56

Chapter Six
The Silence of The Lamb.........................67

Chapter Seven
Is Anybody Listening? The Cry of the Sheep.........................76

Chapter Eight
Wolves In Shepherds' Clothing.........................83

Chapter Nine
Is That What That Scripture Meant? The Integrity of Preaching. 102

Chapter Ten
Who's Covering You? The Accountability In Collegiality.........................122

Epilogue.........................138
Contact the Author.........................141
About the Author.........................143

Prologue
To Fallen Shepherds and Fractured Sheep

It is an undeniable truth that there have been and presently are many fractions and failures within the Church. Contrary to religious deniability and congregational coverups, there exists on this earth no perfect Shepherd and no perfect Sheep. I must admit that in many of these scenarios, these fallings and fractures are due both to bad decisions and undisciplined behaviors that produce wounded perceptions. Wounded perceptions are caused by the teachings of a warped perspective of how things are to function within the Body of Christ and in parallel to the finished works of Christ. This can give birth to the existence of a weary performance from people who produce a religious perversion of wayward practices that is perpetuated through an old wine skin doctrine. When we merge Old Testament Laws with New Testament Truths, without proper hermeneutics and biblical exegeses, cancerous and religious behaviors are birthed.

When Sheep don't know, they look to their Shepherds to provide teachings that will empower them with truths that will work toward their proper levels of spiritual and intellectual growth. However, even in the best of hospitals, mistakes are made, and patients sometimes get wounded. This, however, is the absolute imperfect nature of the human experience and existence. This is why the mercy and grace of God must be understood in its proper context and implemented in how we function within the Body of Christ, and with people in general. I am not going to make excuses for anyone who neglects to use proper biblical integrity for a purpose that benefits their own personal coffers. But I will, however, remind us that the necessity of a love that nurtures and needles us into becoming who God intended for us to become is all spun on the fabric of God's grace.

This controversial writing is a literary exposé of truth, not a legalistic tabloid that exposes the unfortunate failures and flaws that occur so often on the religious landscape. It is not an indictment on any one person or persons, but it is an indicative in-depth confrontation to the non-mentions that have paralyzed the progress of God's kingdom agenda for his people. This is why I dedicate this book to the many Shepherds who have faced public scandals, ridicule, and personal ostracism from the supposed Christian community, which on many occasions forgot about the ministry of restoration. Also I dedicate this book to the many wounded Sheep who left the sheepfold due to offenses that were above their level of spiritual tolerance and maturity. It is an unfortunate neglect that happens in the Church when there are upper-tier leadership scandals. We minister in some ways to the leaders, but we forget about the emotional fractures that impact those humble followers who laid all they had on the line of devotion, loyalty, commitment and trust. To have that trust broken and then to have those wounds ignored are not the way that healing and restoration are supposed to work.

Having been a pastor of three congregations over a span of 37 of the 41 years that I've been in ministry, I know there were those who were offended at times by some of my actions and decisions. When I knew of such cases, I did all that I could to mend those wounds. But for those I didn't know of then, I apologize to them also now. I pray that all who have been hurt and abandoned will find their peace and resolve to understand that to forgive and to be forgiven are not antithetical adversaries, but they are the absolute synopsis of each other and are significant to the experience of grace. My devotion in this book is not to create gossip for critics who see the Church and its pastors through the dark critical and cynical optics of dark-lensed views. I am seeking healing without coverups because no one or no thing can be healed if the cause is not exposed and expelled. We can do better and we must do better because we are better than who many in the world believe and say we are. May Jesus Christ, by the Power of The Holy Spirit, bring restoration, reparation, and revival to His Church and to the world at large.

Acknowledgments

I would be vain and void of good sense and common decency to not pause and pen with gratuitous applause those who have in some way fostered me into where I am at this moment in my life. As I prepare to reach a new milestone and pinnacle in my life, having turned Sixty Years Old. I want to give my regards to certain people by name and others by honorable mention without name.

Let me start by thanking my wife, Pamela, of 38 years for doing her best to keep up with the ever changing dimensions of a man and husband who is constantly evolving and, on most occasions, doing so without explanation nor opportunity for your input. You are a rock solid kind of girl; I love you for your courage and appreciate you for your love and loyalty to our family and me.

To my four children, Raymond, Ashley, Andrea and Carlos Jr. Also, thanks to Andrea, I now have her husband, Derby, my wonderful new son. Your lives give me reason to strive to leave a legacy that will always make you proud to call me Daddy, Father, Pops. You all have opened my eyes and impacted my philosophical thinking in a great way. I have to be a good man and father because your eyes are upon me daily.

To my siblings, Ricardo, Roderick, Veronica, Carmen, Steve, Genyne, Jarrod, who are still here sharing this wonderful life with me, my love for you is undeniable and for eternity and I pray that I've been an example of what I share in this book. To My deceased siblings, Kevin, Roosevelt Jr., and Terry, I pray that when all of this is over, we'll really get to have a real family reunion; God knows my heart has some hollow places because you all are not here.

To my parents, Roosevelt and Mary Lee Malone, I have tried to live up to the standards that you all laid out before my siblings and me. I know that I've missed the mark on many occasions, but I know within my heart that your love and support would've never swayed nor strayed from me. While still living and even now, I feel your presence and discipline in my heart to this very day. I miss You Two, greatly!

To The Bethel Church of Miami, Florida, thank you all for 28 years of support while allowing me to learn how to be a good pastor and teacher. You are the spiritual laboratory that gave birth to my pastoral maturity; I am forever grateful to God to you for your generous care of my family and me.

I give honorable recognition and thanks to my Apostolic Covering and Spiritual Father, Apostle Dr. John Testola. You are a true gift from the Spirit to me, and I honor you as such for the constant impartation that you release into my life weekly and sometimes even daily, even though you live in New York City and travel the globe constantly. You always make time for me; for that I thank you and love you from the depths of my heart.

I also want to pay tribute to the following people who have been a source of spiritual nurturing in my life. Some have gone on to be with The Lord while others still remain here:

Rev. A.L. Gee, who Baptized me at age 6, Licensed me at age 19, and Pastored me for the first 20 years of my life. Rev. Jerome Jackson, who Big Brothered me. Daddy Dr. M.R. Lemons, who Pastored and Ordained me as his first and only Youth Pastor. Dr. John H. Rouse Sr., who Disciplined and Directed me. Rev. Theodore McFarland, Jr., who Mentored me. Dr. Frederick G. Sampson, who Intellectually Inspired me. Dr. Norman E. Owens, Sr., who Lectured me. Dr. Garfield Hubbard Sr., who Believed in me. Pastor Tommie Ringo, who Sowed richly into me. Pastor Jonas Hubbard, who gave me many Opportunities. Pastor Delancey Moore and Pastor Steve Wooten, who stood by me closely as true Brothers and Friends. Dr. Mark Hanby, who Fathered me for a season. Dr. Beverly (Bam) Crawford, who Mothered me. Bishop Noel Jones, who Expanded my theological views and Infused my preaching. Bishop Paul S. Morton Sr., who Consecrated me a Bishop and embraced me as a close confidant. Dr. Guy Williams Sr., who always Encouraged me. Bishops Walter O. Granger, Tommie Triplett and Derek Triplett, who remain Three Trusting Brothers. And to my Two Amigos Pastors, Norman E Owens Jr. and Craig Melvin Smith, who gave me sermonic insights and pushed my levels of confidence. All of these men and women of God are forever etched into who I am today. Some names many of you don't even know, but every one of them were and still remain lights of love and lessons in my life.

To all of my ministry and pastoral Sons, Daughters and Lil Brothers and Sisters, far too many for me to name, you are true validations to my Apostleship, and you all are reasons why this book is a necessity for me to write.

To those of you who remain nameless in this book—not because of some form of mystery, and you all know who you are, and there are so many of you that I don't want to miss anyone, and some of you wouldn't want me to mention your names anyway—thank you for being staples in my life who held me together through some tough times of transition and necessary trade-offs.

In a category all to Himself, I thank God My Father in creation, Jesus my Savior in redemption, and The Holy Spirit my Comforter, Teacher and Guide. I love You and I believe in You without doubt or waver; my walk with you through the writing of this book has proven more to me about what you have placed within me. I thank you for using my ears to hear and my hands to write and my heart to not fear any outcomes as a result of this bold writing. You are the only reason why I exist. Thank You Father God.

May those who find this writing to be edifying, please give God all The Glory and Praise because I'm only the conduit He has chosen to use. The quality of who I am or will ever be is because of his Grace, Mercy and Long-suffering.

INTRODUCTION
TRUTH TO POWER

Predatory practices and seductive schemes of manipulation have almost become the norm within the framework of the relationship between many charismatic preachers and the people to whom they are allowed to minister. Ecclesiastical egocentricity is the classical corruption that controls the mind of many men and women who are supposed to represent God, but they have become self seduced into serving their own bellies. Backroom deals designed to probe the congregation for monies that are not fully for ministry work but for percentage sharing between both speakers and pastor is a sign of no integrity. To think that people do not know that these things exist is to believe that the Holy Spirit does not see these ungodly works and that He does not give discernment to other Spirit-filled people besides pastors and prophets. The God whom we have faith in, we must also have fear of; this is a reverential fear in our hearts that causes us to revere him in great honor.

Sometimes, it is our framework that is our personal blame at work.

When this happens and when it goes unchecked, the Body of Christ is damaged in ways that cause a spiritual cancer that erupts in volumes and spreads. This can cause unhealthy alliances based upon a trust of ignorance because some people honestly believe that some of these predatory men and women of God are genuinely authentic. It has been falsely portrayed that Jesus' metaphoric use of the word *sheep* to describe those who follow pastoral leadership was pointing to the mental posture of ignorance or a simplistic dumbness within the sheep nature. Such is not the case and should never be assumed when it comes to the nature of people who follow our leadership. I have discovered that the biblical content of the Sheep has intellectually increased, and we are seeing that many in the sheepfold are more disciplined to study and consecration than many who occupy the preaching platform.

When I was given the inspiration to write this book in 2012, I was agonized by an apprehensive hesitance because I knew that among many spiritual leaders, there is this non-appreciation for honesty that is referred to as dishonesty within the club of clergy. Many leaders want honor but not honesty, when in fact, honesty is honor. God's inspiration for this writing is to use the gift of this pen and the volume of my voice for the purpose of correction, direction and instruction. I have nothing of my own in terms of motive other than my obedience to Him who has called and anointed me for this work. I have no specific individuals in mind as a reference to my inspired articulated opinions; I am addressing an ideology that has weakened both the effectiveness and influence of the Ecclesiastical and Ecumenical Community.

Allow me to insert into this introduction a disclaimer in my defense and in defense of the many great pastors who are doing great work for the Kingdom of God around the world. There are more good preachers than bad ones in this world; it's just that the bad ones throw a negative light over the good ones. It is common nature in people to see the bad in things more than they do the good, and the media tends to trend toward what sells as opposed to the substance of truth. I will repeat this view in other chapters because I don't want to feed into the narrative of the foolishness of people who say that all preachers are pimps, players and predators. That is not a true claim, and I resent those who ascribe to such views with such vague stereotypical conclusions. If a preacher is financially broke or just average, that doesn't make him authentic; if a preacher obtains wealth legitimately and not manipulatively, that doesn't make him false. This book is not designed to promote gossip, false innuendoes or lies, only truth based on my knowledge of the Word of God and my own personal experiences over the last forty-one years of ministry.

On occasion, I have been blinded by my own interpretive powers and proclivities and have allowed the pleasures of my flesh to temporarily pervert the power of my spiritual influence. Influence in the natural realm is motivated by influence in the spiritual realm. Too much manifestation of our flesh manipulates our spiritual power and can render us ineffective. You see, anything that you can't move to positive change in the spirit realm you won't move in the earth or natural realm. Confession, however, is a key to correction. But because we really don't follow in fullness the Word of God, many of us are ashamed to acknowledge our scars. This happens because the people who follow us admire our stars while never giving consideration to the human scars that tend to influence our better judgments.

It is my hope that those who would be audacious enough to read this book—without the expectation of an apology—would give humble consideration and introspection to expose themselves to themselves and allow God to heal those broken places. Preaching and ministering are so much more effective when we allow ourselves to be transparent, truthful and trusting while God graciously delivers us through all the things that could potentially stagnate the effectiveness of our power. Influence comes with great responsibility, personal initiative, and the intentionality to guard ourselves from personal recklessness. Be mindful that the way God found us is not the way he intended for us to remain. We must embrace both challenge and chastisement, so we can become the reflectors of His glory, grace and goodness.

This book is not written to be a pamphlet of spiritual appeasement and emotional pampering, but it is designed to disturb and disrupt the psychology of your religious tenets, which may be at the core of a personal conflict with the deity who called and commissioned you. You will notice that some chapters are longer than others, but the motive behind discussing these delicate matters is not just to make or prove a point, but also to point us toward change. It is not my desire just to talk about what's wrong, but to offer solutions as a remedy that can re-route the Body of Christ to real and radical changes. So go ahead, be my guest, and eat from these life-preserving and life-saving words that I strongly believe to be the inspired dictates of the Holy Spirit. God Bless You and may you walk in the Truth and Power of God's calling on your life.

Carlos L. Malone, Sr.

CHAPTER ONE

THE CALL VERSUS COMPROMISE

The call of God is the most creditable initiative that God takes toward mankind, other than the redemptive initiative that created the opportunity for salvation based on the atonement and finished works of Christ. Being called of God is a humbling experience because those who are called clearly understand that meritorious honor is not the reason behind the call. When God calls, He calls only on those who trust him and those whom He can trust. From God's perspective, He knows every flaw and future failure of those He calls. The greatest contribution and compliment to your character is the endorsement attached to the assignments given to you by the divine designation of God the Creator. When you know with absolute certainty that you have been called of God, you should welcome that call with impeccable integrity and consent—and with undying commitment.

When most of us are called of God to do a specific assignment, it appears as though that call comes at the most inopportune time and season in our lives. For me, I had to contend with the chaff not yet totally removed from my life, so I hoped that at the least I would have perfected my character to a place of spotless living. Now compound that with the reality that the call into ministry was nowhere on my radar of career opportunities. The truth beyond my own personal trappings is this: it didn't take me long to realize that the call of God was authentic just as the struggles in my life were authentic competitive struggles. Please understand that the struggles that I faced at that time were on so many different levels and layers of insecurities and fears. That was the reality of the call that I had to face. And because of the many religious denominational influences in my life, it made my struggle even harder. When you know more about the power of your struggles than you do about the person and power of God, it empowers the struggle set against you even more. Back then I did not understand anything about purpose and process or about how these channels are tools that God uses to perfect who we're becoming. Now we understand that God's process of us is a reflection of the transitions that it takes for us to become who He has already pre-determined in eternity past to become in eternity future. Our focus must be to remain in steadfast discipline to the divine design and desire of God for our lives and not allow counterfeit assignments to tempt us away from that.

> **When you know more about the power of your struggles than you do about the person and power of God, it empowers the struggle set against you even more.**

Because of a principle of truth that I have learned that say's everything taken for God must be tested by God, I am not surprised by the swaying tactics of the enemy to short circuit our success cycle by persuasive powers of influence that could lead us down the paths of compromise. Now, compromise is a strategic offering of alternative facts that attempts to alter the truth of a standard that you have embraced or a promise that you have been given. Compromise strives to get you to contradict the dictates that have been directly given to you to follow. Compromise is doing something totally antithetical to that which you have committed yourself. Compromise is taking less for something that is worth more. And this is the message communicated in this chapter.

When you study the temptation narratives of Jesus in the wilderness, you discover that this spiritual cosmic collision between the powers of a spiritual deity and a demonic entity was to get Jesus, in human flesh and without divine prerogatives, either to stick to the assignment given or to compromise for the alternatives presented. The attacker in this narrative is appealing to a season of vulnerability of the assigned person of Jesus.

The season was 40 days of fasting and isolation, after which God instructed Jesus to go into the wilderness to be tested. The tempter delayed his attack until the assigned appeared to show delayed vulnerability. **It is important for us to always remember that the cracks of deterioration will always come just before the crumbling of destruction.** Showing vulnerability in plain view becomes the voice that invites the vicious attacks of the enemy from within and without.

> Then was Jesus led up of the Spirit into the wilderness to be tempted of the devil. And when he had fasted forty days and forty nights, he was afterward hungered. And when the tempter came to him, he said, "If thou be the son of God, command that these stones be made bread." — Matthew 4:1–3

Notice how the enemy in the narrative strategically appeals to the potential uncertainty he thinks Jesus might have about being the Son of God. So he tries to pull Jesus into an egocentric proving of himself. But Jesus knowing himself and knowing that he did not come to serve his ego but to suffer the agony of the cross, he plays Bible trivia about what God says with the enemy as opposed to proving who he is. If we remain conscious of what God says during our times of testing, we will experience what God has promised in our hour of testing—victory without defeat.

> **Compromise always appeals to your lower nature, but it is designed to interrupt and disrupt your higher calling.**

Compromise always appeals to your lower nature, but it is designed to interrupt and disrupt your higher calling. Your awareness of the nature and magnitude of the call of God on your life must be an unsettled issue in your psychological and emotional propensities. You must know the value of who you are to God if you're going to defeat the voices of compromise that are perpetually creating opportunities of distractions in your life. Your vulnerabilities can get you to commit a violation against your value, especially if you do not understand the significance of the nature and magnitude of God's call. When He called you, He had a plan and a purpose for that call. If you decide to cross pollenate his plans with substituted suggestions that only play to your egocentric cadences, then you are headed for a disastrous ending. It is to be understood that whenever the enemy comes to destroy, he is never thinking short-term damage, which gives you room for ultimate recovery. He is always thinking about life-time destruction, which leaves no room for recovery or restoration. Therefore, he will stack up points of power over you during a period of time, making you think you have gotten away with those indiscretions. And when the time is right for him—but wrong for you—he'll drop that nuclear bomb on you. It's never only a single bullet that impacts you, but a bomb that is designed and aimed to cause destruction to your entire sphere of influence.

So a conversation is needed right here and now, which demands the imposition of questions that you must answer for and within yourself:

1. **What does the call of God on my life mean to me in terms of value?**

2. **How do I consider the call of God on my life when facing potential violations that contradict my claim to being called? What human excuses do I make for myself?**

3. **As a result of the call of God on my life, do I consider myself a victim because of the mandated restraints imposed upon my human will?**

4. **How often do I honestly validate the violations that I commit that are antithetical to my core spiritual beliefs?**

5. **Do I ever compare the volume of my virtuous behavior to the vices that I surrender to, which I know are out of bounds according to the Word of God?**

6. **Do I value my victories more than my defeats? If so, how do I use those victories to be victorious over potential future defeats?**

7. **Do I suffer from the need for validation in my life?** *This can be a vulnerable crack in your spiritual armor.*

I tried to dutifully and honestly understand the Holy Spirit's line of questioning here because I began to feel personally exposed. This is good because it means many of you may experience an imposing pressure on you too as you read these questions for yourself. I have intentionally avoided providing answers or suggestions to the above questions because

I want to open up the windows of your soul, so you can have a transparent conversation with yourself. Don't be embarrassed. Know that truth confronted and claimed is a lie controlled and conquered. Embrace your truth and face your embarrassment with the reality that you are victorious beyond anything and everything you may have done that has not been in the will of God for your life. There are no warrants out for your arrest, only for your unrest. There is no way for you to be both a Spirit-filled person and be at peace with the flawed failures of a called man or woman of God. God wants you at rest with Him, so He can perform his greater work through you.

Compromising your call is not a proper tribute to the investment God has made in you, and it is an uneven exchange that signals you'd rather trade off counterfeit over authentic, cheap over expensive, failure over success and death over life. Living your life under the pressure of a double standard that inflicts mental and emotional judgments and paranoia is not God's plan for your life. You were called and commissioned to do what will glorify God, horrify the demon world and edify the human one. Walk in true devotion to that call and beware of those delegate moments in which compromise is a masque in disguise with only one plan to create disconnect between you and the voice of He who called you. No matter what's being offered, it's not worth the take. Whatever you give into it, you can rest assured it will come to take more than what you got from it. Be wise and know that your worth and your true wealth is at stake every day that you are given life. Fight with diligence and faith and with the attitude that no weapon formed against you can prosper. Give no power to your enemies by not yielding your flesh to the works of the enemy. **Compromise is a cheap trick, but an expensive trap!**

> **Know that truth confronted and claimed is a lie controlled and conquered. Embrace your truth and face your embarrassment with the reality that you are victorious beyond anything and everything you may have done that has not been in the will of God for your life.**

CHAPTER TWO

WHOSE SHEEP ARE THEY ANYWAY?

Intentions without proper instructions and understanding can lead to premature conclusions about a particular matter. And once those intentions are called into question, the matter at hand must be able to face irrefutable evidence. Such questioning is often imposed intentionally to target the men and women who serve as pastors over local church assemblies. These include Senior Pastors, Ministry Pastors, or any other Subjacent Pastor who serve within the local assembly of God. In light of such questioning of Church shepherds, we must then ask the obvious question of whose sheep are these who assemble together voluntarily to give support to the local church assembly? The answer to this question will expose the mental posture of those who have been graciously given the opportunity to serve in the house of God. Let me say unapologetically that the Church—and all that it is called to be—is God's by ownership, and the care of it is given to pastors or shepherds by stewardship. Having the proper perspective about this very ideal will prevent the egocentric perversion and the iconic idolatrous imagery that is parading the pulpit platform throughout the religious community.

The illusion of the mega church, in many cases, has given birth to a confused and misrepresented ideology of God's intent for the Body of

Christ. Men have overrated themselves in God's plan and intention for calling and placing them over His flocks. We are only conduits for God's use and His glory. We are not to be crowns of control over the heads of the sheep that require, at times, a perverted loyalty that is sickening at its core. Often, drawing the crowd's attractions to us can send a message to our egos that can make us believe our own self-invented hype about ourselves; this can become a hallucinogenic to our perceptions of who we are. God doesn't need us, but He chooses to use us, so we should always be mindful of this as we give attentive care to the sheepfold. The obvious answer to the question of whose sheep are they is very simple—they all belong to God. The Bible teaches us this principle, and all we have to do is be mindful of it. The Gospel of John, chapter ten, gives an excellent biblical discourse of this truth:

The Good Shepherd and His Sheep

"I tell you the truth, anyone who sneaks over the wall of a sheepfold, rather than going through the gate, must surely be a thief and a robber! But the one who enters through the gate is the shepherd of the sheep. The gatekeeper opens the gate for him, and the sheep recognize his voice and come to him. He calls his own sheep by name and leads them out. After he has gathered his own flock, he walks ahead of them, and they follow him because they know his voice. They won't follow a stranger; they will run from him because they don't know his voice." Those who heard Jesus use this illustration didn't understand what he meant, so he explained it to them: "I tell you the truth, I am the gate for the sheep. All who came before me were thieves and robbers. But the true sheep did not listen to them. Yes, I am the gate. Those who come in through me will be saved. They will come and go freely and will find good pastures. The thief's purpose is to steal and kill and destroy. My purpose is to give them a rich and satisfying life. I am the good shepherd. The good shepherd sacrifices his life for the sheep. A hired hand will run when he sees a wolf coming. He will abandon the sheep because they don't belong to him and he isn't their shepherd. And so the wolf attacks them and scatters the flock. The hired hand runs away because he's working only for the money and doesn't really care about the sheep. I am the good shepherd; I know my own sheep, and they know me, just as my Father knows me and I know the Father. So I sacrifice my life for the sheep." — John 10:1–15, NLT

The distinctions between the true Shepherd and a mere thief can't be anymore clearer than in this biblical text. By holding on to this Scripture, I am able to subject myself to the truth as spoken by Jesus himself, and this keeps me from developing an unhealthy alliance to the sheep that I have leadership over. To this end, in the next two subsections, I define descriptively the role and the rules of both shepherd and sheep. Hence, I want to ensure that understanding and clarity punctuate the framework of these two biblical roles.

Practical Principles that Govern the Shepherd and the Sheep:

Shepherds must be...

Serving: The word *serving* has nearly become the lost treasure within the ranks of pastoral ministry, and it has had a trickle down affect on the congregation at large. It is now a struggle to find people in church with a servant's heart. We live in a time when elevation of position has created the elimination of humility and servanthood. Men and women in ministry have become celebrated celebrities. Unfortunately, as a result, they have become celibate to serving. Many of them find certain aspects of a humble nature to be beneath their dignitary status. I have seen many such "dignitaries," who claim to be shepherds, treat their sheepfold with such arrogant abuse and condescending demeanor. As pastors, **we are called to serve the least of the sheep, not only the elite of the fold** because we find benefit from them. Personally, serving people to the glory of God has been my most distinguished honor because it is through that service that I've come to understand the depth of God's love for me when He sent his Son to die for my vileness.

Washing of Feet

> Jesus knew that the Father had given him authority over everything and that he had come from God and would return to God. So he got up from the table, took off his robe, wrapped a towel around his waist, and poured water into a basin. Then he began to wash the disciples' feet, drying them with the towel he had around him. When Jesus came to Simon Peter, Peter said to him, "Lord, are you going to wash my feet?" Jesus replied, "You don't understand now what I am doing, but someday you will." "No," Peter protested, "you will never ever wash my feet!" Jesus replied, "Unless I wash you, you won't belong to me." Simon Peter exclaimed, "Then wash my hands and head as well, Lord, not just my feet!" — John 13:3–9 NLT

Serving is synonymous to power and a healthy influence on the people whom we are called to lead. Jesus set the example in the preceding biblical text because he proved that he knew who he was. He knew what he possessed. He knew who his enemies were, but yet he served them any way, and he refused to allow anyone to elevate him where only his Father could place him. This is the attitude that all pastors must have. We must remain in the spirit of a servant throughout our ministry tenure. Don't allow your titles to take you where a testimony of humility can't control you.

Sacrificing: One of the attributes of serving is sacrifice—the offering of one's self, substance and resources to a cause that benefits others more than yourself. It is the surrendering gladly of your gain to the good of others, even if nothing is left over for yourself. When assuming the role of a shepherd, we must demonstrate a posture that reflects that of the ultimate Shepherd, Jesus Christ—the Good Shepherd. Anyone who is not the reflective personification of him is an imposter—overrated and undeserving of both title and position. Pastoring requires a level of sacrifice that must never be in competition with a selfish will or self-centered agenda. From the shepherd's perspective, shepherding sheep is about the sheep more than it is about the shepherd.

The unfortunate reality—within the context of the present-day interpretation of what it means to be a contemporary pastor and church—is that sacrificing of one's self has become an antiquated ideology, eclipsed by entitlement to fame, fortune and front row acceptance. This is an appetite that desires no initial investment of a life of devotion and honor towards being called of God to serve His people. The joy of pastoring is the joy that comes from pastoring; it is the shared engagement of pastor and people together engulfed in the growth cycle with God. Pastors are expected to be willing to sacrifice certain parts of their lives for the good and advancement of God's people. The motive of the pastor must always be in sync with the mandate of the pastor. That mandate must never be interrupted or altered in any way by anything that deflects away from God's initial intent. The John 10 narrative that I shared at the beginning of this chapter is reflected in these thoughts and ideals. Pastoring is a ministry of sacrifice, and it should never be placed in the hands of hirelings who become predatory parasites who come to do selfish harm to the sheep.

Elevation now happens by the power of sacrifice. When you sacrifice for God, He will supply you with everything you need—if you're willing to endure the longevity of the process. The Apostle Paul, in writing to the Galatians in chapter six verse nine, encourages us not to get weary in doing well because we are to reap if we do not faint or lose heart. It is important to understand the nature of the sacrifices that God requires of those whom He chooses to serve in pastoral roles. God is not asking you to physically die for His sheep, but He does expect you to live in sacrificial service to the advancement of the Kingdom of God. Now, if for the sake of righteousness you have to protect the sheep, God will sustain you in doing so. Remember that we are not called to war against an enemy of flesh and blood, but we are called to confront the spiritually demonic principalities and powers that engage us in spiritual combat. **The harvest you will reap will always be greater than the sacrifices you make.**

The joy of pastoring is the joy that comes from pastoring; it is the shared engagement of pastor and people together engulfed in the growth cycle with God.

Sensitive: Being sensitive is not a suggestion to be simple or soft, but it is a consciousness of focused compassion that is attentive to the needs of God's people. It's catering without compromise and discipline with a devotion that intentionally targets the positive development of God's people. Sometimes, a pulpit brash battering that is borderline emotional abuse is conveyed in the message presentation. Governing people in the context of ministry service is guiding people to their best resolve within the context of the biblical mandate. Personal opinions are never to be the isolated instructions given to God's people. We must adhere to the Scriptures at all times without compromise, even when situations are of a conflicting nature. As a pastor with 36 years of pastoral experience—4 years at one church, another 4 years at another, and 28 years and counting at the current—I have made it my safety net to govern according to the Word of God, even when existing church bylaws were used to contradicted biblical instruction. I made it my mission and the church's mandate to bring the church in line with the Word of God. Now trust me when I tell you that I received resistance in some of those churches, but the Word of God wins every time.

> Only be thou strong and very courageous, that thou mayest observe to do according to all the law, which Moses my servant commanded thee: turn not from it to the right hand or to the left, that thou mayest prosper whithersoever thou goest. This book of the law shall not depart out of thy mouth; but thou shalt meditate therein day and night, that thou mayest observe to do according to all that is written therein: for then thou shalt make thy way prosperous, and then thou shalt have good success. Have not I commanded thee? Be strong and of a good courage; be not afraid, neither be thou dismayed: for the Lord thy God is with thee whithersoever thou goest. — Joshua 1:7–9

> And I will give you shepherds after my own heart, who will guide you with knowledge and understanding. — Jeremiah 3:15, NLT

> The shepherds of my people have lost their senses. They no longer seek wisdom from the Lord. Therefore, they fail completely, and their flocks are scattered. — Jeremiah 10:21, NLT

> And Jesus went about all the cities and villages, teaching in their synagogues, and preaching the gospel of the kingdom, and healing every sickness and every disease among the people. But when he saw the multitudes,

he was moved with compassion on them, because they fainted, and were scattered abroad, as sheep having no shepherd. — Matthew 9:35–36

The Bible is very clear in regards to the sensitivity of focus and the steadfast adherence to following the biblical format of guiding and governing God's people. Whenever we get away from pastoring God's way, we are guilty of an obstruction of duty and desire, and we fall into error and are forced to deal with the repercussions and resistances that derive from a flesh-centered ideology. Again, I say, the sheep belong to God; they are His, and we must carry the burden of responsibility on our shoulders because that's what shepherds who are called of God do. However, this works both ways—shepherd to sheep and sheep to shepherd. Each have a responsibility of biblical instructions to follow, and there should be no compromise regarding this matter.

SHEEP MUST BE…..

Taught to Know and Trust the Shepherd: One of the most valuable connections between the shepherd and sheep is a connection that is built on trust. Trust is the undying confidence that is developed between two people or entities that allows for the existence of a reliable expectancy. Trust must be built, not bought; it must be pure, not compromising—even when it is tested because it will be. Trust must be the front and rear view focus that keeps violations at a minimum. As a pastor, I have found that **transparency is a trial, and the trail and that leads to a path of un-perverted trust**. Volunteered information from the shepherd that shows some humanity is mostly valued by the people who it's shared with. I'm not saying totally to expose everything personal, but people truly need to know you are human. Jesus, in his humanity, was tempted in ways like we are, and it made him sensitive to the struggles of men, even though he committed no sin. Knowing that he, the Son of God, felt the same emotional struggles that we feel, encourages my faith in him. Trust in a relationship must be built not solely on stars of perfection, but on scars of imperfection. If not, then it is pretentious and conditional. In order to maintain trust, both the shepherd and

> **Trust in a relationship must be built not solely on stars of perfection, but on scars of imperfection. If not, then it is pretentious and conditional.**

sheep must value that trust at all times and avoid potential circumstances that would cause that trust to become vulnerable and ultimately violated.

When it comes to making decisions within the context of the pastor and his people, along with the direction of the local assembly, open dialogue must be permitted under the guidance of respect for authority and respect for those under authority. Pastors are teachers, not just preachers, therefore, they must teach their people how to follow leadership and vision. Vision is the focus initiative of a ministry or congregation, and it must be made clear to those who are expected to follow it.

> I will stand upon my watch, and set me upon the tower, and will watch to see what he will say unto me, and what I shall answer when I am reproved. And the Lord answered me, and said, "Write the vision, and make it plain upon tables, that he may run that readeth it. For the vision is yet for an appointed time, but at the end it shall speak, and not lie: though it tarry, wait for it; because it will surely come, it will not tarry." — Habakkuk 2:1–3

Vision is both a benchmark and landmark that gives punctuating expression and clarity, so the sheep know how to interpret the intentional goals set by the shepherd. You should never expect people to reach or respond favorably to what you don't teach them to do.

Tender of Tone and Temperament: Being tender with people is a necessity in the nurturing process of dealing with the people whom God gives us responsibility over. Now, I do know that personality plays a part in the scheme of pastoral selection, that is why pastors should be appointed by the spiritual guidance of men and women who have the apostolic grace of God on their life. It should not be made by some board that is impressed by a resume. This is a biblical method that will help ensure that a congregation gets the right leader to cover and guide them. Matured eyes of discernment are able to see into the heart and nature of potential pastorate candidates to determine their true character. When Paul and Barnabas were being considered for their first missionary journey, the apostles/elders prayed and stated these words:

> Now there were in the church that was at Antioch certain prophets and teachers; as Barnabas, and Sime-

on that was called Niger, and Lucius of Cyrene, and Manaen, which had been brought up with Herod the tetrarch, and Saul. As they ministered to the Lord, and fasted, the Holy Ghost said, "Separate me Barnabas and Saul for the work whereunto I have called them." And when they had fasted and prayed, and laid their hands on them, they sent them away. So they, being sent forth by the Holy Ghost, departed unto Seleucia; and from thence they sailed to Cyprus. — Acts 13:1–4

The Council's Letter to Gentile Believers

Then pleased it the apostles and elders, with the whole church, to send chosen men of their own company to Antioch with Paul and Barnabas; namely, Judas surnamed Barsabas, and Silas, chief men among the brethren: And they wrote letters by them after this manner; The apostles and elders and brethren send greeting unto the brethren which are of the Gentiles in Antioch and Syria and Cilicia: Forasmuch as we have heard, that certain which went out from us have troubled you with words, subverting your souls, saying, Ye must be circumcised, and keep the law: to whom we gave no such commandment: It seemed good unto us, being assembled with one accord, to send chosen men unto you with our beloved Barnabas and Paul, Men that have hazarded their lives for the name of our Lord Jesus Christ. We have sent therefore Judas and Silas, who shall also tell you the same things by mouth. For it seemed good to the Holy Ghost, and to us, to lay upon you no greater burden than these necessary things. — Acts 15:22–28

I reference these Scriptures because they take into account the wisdom of spiritually matured men who were led by the Holy Ghost. It also shows how leaders were held to an accountability of both message and mission; this protects both the leader and followers.

Hostility is not a fruit of the Spirit, and it is not a helpful virtue when you are building trust with people. In fact it is a negative inoculation that builds distrustful discord that works against the spiritual health and maturation of the people in the sheepfold. Some pastors have the tendency to adapt a leadership style that is hard and harsh, driven by an insecurity that makes it difficult for people to trust them. Abusive articulation in preaching from the pulpit is a trend in some churches. I do believe that preaching must involve exhortation as well as rebuke, but that rebuke must be done under the guidance of the Holy Spirit, not hostility and harshness.

Trusting the shepherd these days has become a hard challenge for people in today's society because of the negative exposures that find their way into the realm of social media. Being in touch with the sheep and being touched by the sheep are significant to the continuity and connection of trust. Unfortunately, we are living in the era of the iconic class clergy ideology in which the preacher is more celebrity than servant. The untouchable shepherd who is so self-exalted that the sheep can't touch him or her is an abomination to the ministry that Jesus gave to us. While honoring a pastor should never be minimized, it must not be maximized above his or her humility and servanthood. If you are a shepherd, then you should smell like sheep; your connection to your people should not be over guarded. Many have become so arrogant in this area that it has wounded the very perception of the pastor or preacher. No shepherd has to be protected from his sheep to the point where he is untouchable to them. This phenomenon has become a blatant disgust, so I will continue to explore in this book some of the nuances not considered to be the norm. These are the Lord's sheep, so they should be treated as such, and pastors should be acting as such too.

> The untouchable shepherd who is so self-exalted that the sheep can't touch him or her is an abomination to the ministry that Jesus gave to us.

Taught to Know the True Shepherd's Voice by Knowing His Word: In the John ten narrative, Jesus makes it clear that he is the Good Shepherd because he was giving his life for the sheep. He also states that the good shepherd knows his sheep and is known of and by his sheep. With that truth at the core of today's shepherd/pastor understanding, it should be a mandate to raise the people given into our care not just to know our voices alone, but to know the voice of he who gave his life for them. I did not die for the sheep—Jesus did. Some eschatological implications are made by Jesus in this text as he references other sheep not of this fold whom he must bring with him. Ultimately, there will be one fold and one

Shepherd, and this will consist of the sheep who know him experientially and educationally through the teaching of the scriptures and the testimonial encounters that the sheep have with him.

Preaching to arouse emotional responses is not enough in the spiritual health diet of the sheep; edification through the Word and impartation by the Spirit must be top priorities. We must teach the sheep to have an independent ear to hear and know God, through Jesus, for themselves. Jesus is the door through which people must access God. Why? Because he gave his life to redeem mankind by atoning for man's sins. It is not enough to have people hear and know us. They must also know and hear him, so when we speak to them, they will know that the instructions given to us for them are of God. Congregational illiteracy, as it relates to the Bible, is very high within most churches. People come in and out of our churches, but they are not held accountable to being taught and challenged to learn. So much burden is lifted from the local pastor when his people are taught not to be dependent on him but on their relationship with God. You cannot be their personal Bible dictionary or commentary on a daily basis; they must take a deeper interest and invest in increasing their knowledge. This is neither to your advantage as a pastor, nor should it be to your insecurity that aims to keep your people submitted to you by keeping them uninformed in the Word of God.

It has always been and always will be my aim to teach people to be strong believers by pushing them more toward God and less in drawing them toward me. They are a stewardship responsibility that I have, so I must prepare them to meet their creator and savior, which is not me. Empowering people to live fully in their knowledge of God is a great freedom. The Bible says it is the truth that makes us free; it implies that it is the truth that we know that makes us free. Teaching and training people to know the voice of God cannot be emphasized enough; it is the will of God, and it must be the desired will of every shepherding pastor.

Tempered in a way that brings out the best in them: This key component brings endurance and strength to the character of those whom we have oversight responsibility. People may come into the sheepfold weak, but they must be made strong and lasting because they must face the wolves of the world that come to steal, kill and destroy them. Spiritual growth is a maturing process by which people are empowered by their knowledge of the Word of God. The Bible teaches us to know those who labor among us; this is significant to the growth of both the shepherd and sheep. To know something is an intentional discipline and strategy that incorporates a system of responsibility and accountability of effort and efficiency. Managing effectively the people whom we pastor must be a passion-driven initiative that focuses on people's growth as a priority, not just their giving. We must make the sheep better by ensuring that we have opportunities that challenge and track their growth. Now, I know that some of this information may appear repetitious, but that's intentional because I don't want it to become rhetoric that you don't remember or consider, and cast off.

To conclude this chapter, please be mindful that as a shepherd, you are a steward who leads God's children, not an owner who lords over God's people. Guard your heart with humility and see your servitude attitude as an upgrade to your character, not a downgrade to your honor. It is an honor to serve God and His people, and if you do it faithfully, the true owner will definitely reward you for your service to Him. Even though David and his son Solomon were not pastors but kings, the principle of oversight of God's people remains the same. The closing Scripture is a prayer offered by Solomon regarding the wisdom and integrity of how he should rule and reign over God's people. I love this prayer and it should also be a prayer of principles that should be offered by all leaders of people. The rich shepherd, poor sheep message is one that mandates the equity of sharing prosperity for all of God's children, not just to be kept by those at the top.

> Give your love of justice to the king, O God, and righteousness to the king's son. Help him judge your people in the right way; let the poor always be treated fairly. May the mountains yield prosperity for all, and may the hills be fruitful. Help him to defend the poor, to rescue the children of the needy, and to crush their oppressors. May they fear you as long as the sun shines, as long

as the moon remains in the sky. Yes, forever! May the king's rule be refreshing like spring rain on freshly cut grass, like the showers that water the earth. May all the godly flourish during his reign. May there be abundant prosperity until the moon is no more. — Psalm 72:1–7, NLT

CHAPTER THREE

Lead Them, Feed Them, But Don't Need Them

One particular narrative necessitates a conversation of considerable confronting. This narrative oftentimes reflects a hidden emotional and psychological need that manipulates the agenda motive of some pastoral leadership behavior. This entanglement of misdiagnosed intentions has caused many pastors to bleed for need from the people whom they are called to lead. The expectancy from the shepherd of the sheep can foster a spirit of rejection and/or rebellion, which disrupts the core of assumption shepherds have regarding the manner by which the sheep respond to him or her. As theoretical or assumptive as this may sound to some, it has become a truth of record within my 37 years of pastoral experience and exposure. I have counseled and advised many pastors who have fallen into the trap of overrated expectation as it relates to how the people respond to them. In the previous chapter, I reminded us of whose sheep these are that we shepherd; in the context of truth, they belong to God, but we find many pastors who assume the sheep are theirs. If you understand that they are not yours, but God's, then your aim will always remain integral to the idea that you must never develop an ownership posture over the sheep you lead.

As shockingly awkward and out of bounds as this may sound, a magnitude of personal insecurities exist as a yoke of control within the emotions of some pastors. Many of these insecurities go unchecked and unnoticed because many people are under the false assumption that God calls perfect men and women to serve in these capacities of leadership. Oftentimes, these expectations are religious in their content, but they do not in any way comply with biblical reality. It is my intent to expose the truth, not the lies, that suggests preachers and pastors are super strong icons with flawless character traits. Some will try and publicly project these pretentious personas, but in the reality of their life scope, it's not true. God doesn't need perfect people in order to do a perfect work through them. Every good thing we possess as people, we possess them not by our own works, but by the abundance of grace that God gives us to do this work He calls us to do. Should we strive for perfection? Yes, we should. Will we ever be perfect? No, we won't—or as Doc Holiday, portrayed by Val Kilmer in the classic western *Tombstone*, said, "You're a daisy if you do."

> **God doesn't need perfect people in order to do a perfect work through them. Every good thing we possess as people, we possess them not by our own works, but by the abundance of grace that God gives us to do this work He calls us to do.**

Let's consider some potential needs that capture the focus of many pastors, causing them to become vulnerable to an obsession of need from their sheep. The things I share here are not to suggest there exists some kind of perverted or erotic underlying need between shepherds and sheep. I am bringing to light only some well-needed conversation, so healthy relationships and helpful resources can assist pastors in how they deal with God's sheep.

THE NEED FOR ACCEPTANCE AND APPROVAL

Whenever a pastor is assigned or called to a local assembly, there exists within that pastor a desire to see his leadership as an opportunity for success. No pastor wants to fail at doing his or her job; it is, therefore, a natural inclination to see things work and move in a positive direction. Many suggested ideas are shared with pastors about what the proper approach should be in their new assignments. I believe that one size doesn't fit all when dealing with the sheepfold; however, I do believe that one God and His Spirit does rule all. Every pastoral assignment should be made in heaven and released on earth, not made on earth and then offered up for God to cosign. God is responsible only for what he assigns us, not for what we sign up. God always approves us before He even proves us when He calls us to an assignment. He makes his decisions concerning our assignments after the counsel of his own will, not the selection of some church board committee. This is why a man or woman of God should consult God before ever taking a pastoral assignment. Every good opportunity is not a God opportunity, regardless of the material benefits that come with the offer.

Whenever I was confident the assignment I had taken was a God sanction on my life, that changed the narrative and the nature of my focus. It is within this context that I govern the people to whom He sent me and also myself. This has been the stable confidence that has guided me to understand that no matter how smart I may think I am concerning the mode and mood of people, God has always been my source of reference. The nature or attitude of people should never be the framework by which we function among them. God knows his people, and I am totally submitted in both love and loyalty to taking them in the direction that God instructs, not the desire of their will. I do know there are psychological tenets that we are tempted to use to get the best results from people, but sometimes people can desire one thing but need something totally different. By nature, I am a people person and I love sensitively hard; however, I've had to protect myself from my need to be accepted and approved by them. You see, when you've been approved by God, it doesn't matter if the people approve or accept you as long as they respect and honor you. You will discover that if you don't compromise, God will move on the hearts of the people and will, through your obedience to his Word, affirm who you are in their midst. Stop trying to get from them what you need to feel secure in your position, and give them what God knows they need, and let that give you both confidence and comfort.

> **God always approves us before He even proves us when He calls us to an assignment. He makes his decisions concerning our assignments after the counsel of his own will, not the selection of some church board committee.**

Let's consider some biblical narratives, so you can see how men like Moses, Joshua, Saul and David handled themselves as leaders of God's people. Through these biblical accounts, you will see how approval and acceptance from people compare emotionally to approval and acceptance by God. Religion-based and fan-based leadership that seeks to please people and personal agendas are antithetical to the design and desires of God. These biblical narratives are too long for me to list in their total presentation, but I will reference them for your research and summarize them for their presentation in this chapter. The ultimate point of this is to show those of you who read this book that you can't allow yourselves to be taken hostage to a need for acceptance and approval from people. God is calling people to himself, not to you or me, and we must at all times accept and protect God's way as ours. God does assign people to us, but He calls them to himself, and he uses us to assist in getting them to him.

Moses

Moses was a great leader, a man of apostolic and prophetic powers, but he became attached to the people he led and was, oftentimes, influenced emotionally and psychologically by their response and lack thereof to him. He took their actions personally instead of professionally and prophetically while maintaining a proper perspective concerning them. He listened to their murmuring and was, at times, bitter by their disobedience. The reality is they were not his sheep, but they were God's people, called of Him to do His work in His kingdom. What Moses did was interpret the people's disobedience as a rebellion not only against God but as though it was against him too. Moses' assignment was to lead the children of Israel to the Promised Land as God had instructed. He got too emotionally engaged and attached his mental compass and responses to how they responded to him.

What Moses did was interpret the people's disobedience as a rebellion not only against God but as though it was against him too.

Moses goes up Mt. Sinai to receive God's instructions. In Exodus chapter thirty-two, the people became restless because of the many days and nights that Moses was gone. They began turning to a form of idolatry and built for themselves a golden calf to worship. God tells Moses of His dissatisfaction with His people and tells him to get down unto them because they have truly angered Him. In verse ten of Exodus thirty-two, God is specific in telling Moses, **"Now therefore let me alone, that my wrath may wax hot against them, and that I may consume them: and I will make of thee a great nation."** After God makes this decision,

Moses calms God down. In verse fourteen, the Bible says, **"And the Lord repented of the evil which he thought to do unto his people."** Now what happens next is proof of Moses' warped idea of how to deal with these people who belonged to God. So he comes down Sinai with the two tablets inscribed with God's writing on both sides of them. He is met by Joshua. And when Joshua hears the noise from camp, he assumes it is war, but Moses knows, based on what God had told him, that it is the noise of sin and revelry. Now watch how he totally flips once he sees what they are doing in verses nineteen through twenty: **"And it came to pass, as soon as he came nigh unto the camp, that he saw the calf, and the dancing: and Moses' anger waxed hot, and he cast the tablets out of his hands, and brake them beneath the mount. And he took the calf which they had made, and burnt it in the fire, and ground it to powder, and strawed it upon the water, and made the children of Israel drink of it."**

> These are God's people, and they should never be a source of acceptance or approval that defines and determines how you handle what God gives you to do.

You can now clearly see my point. Moses initially didn't want God to judge his people, so he spoke up in favor of them. But when he saw for himself what they were doing, he gets so mad that he destroyed everything God had given him while he was in the mountain for forty days fasting. Pastors, please understand that you can't be so invested emotionally with God's people that you let your emotional investment make you ignore your ultimate assignment. These are God's people, and they should never be a source of acceptance or approval that defines and determines how you handle what God gives you to do. Moses ended up having at least three thousand men slaughtered that day. Now he has to go back to God and make intercession again for their sins; he even tells God that if He won't forgive their sins, then to erase his name from out of the records of His writings. He is so in love with these people, but they are not his. As pastors we are sometimes more affectionate about God's wife and children than we are about our own. But like the saying that I have said, "I am not dying for another man's wife." Lead them, feed them but don't need them in a way that misdirects your judgment. They are not there to ascribe to your emotional needs; they are given to you for you to lead them into a deeper relationship with God, so they can meet His acceptance and approval. They need to know what the good, perfect and acceptable will of God is—don't you go around peddling for some kind of need supply for yourself. In the end, Moses ended up only seeing the Promised Land, but never entering it because his anger at the people pushed him over the ledge of obedience to God into disobedience. He struck the rock more times than he was instructed, and God altered his ending, even though he was still favored by God and served with great fervor and endurance. He was just too emotionally and psychologically invested in God's people, and it cost him greatly. The question becomes what are you willing to lose by holding falsely onto that which does not belong to you?

JOSHUA

Joshua was a different kind of leader. We see him as having a much more controlled and disciplined temperament than his predecessor Moses. Joshua had witnessed firsthand the ramifications of being pulled out of focus by the people whom one leads. He understood that his allegiance had to be more to his assignment and assignor, not the people to whom he was assigned. He understood he had to love them in order to lead them, but he wasn't leading them to love themselves; they had a lover, and Joshua understood he was not that lover. Joshua was commanded to remain focused and attentive to the instructions of God and to the law as it was written. He had the assurance of God that he would be protected by and provided for by Him. His allegiance to the assignment would bring great dividends from God.

As shepherds of sheep, we have to look totally to God to protect and provide for us; we must not put the total burden on the sheep.

As shepherds of sheep, we have to look totally to God to protect and provide for us; we must not put the total burden on the sheep. I also do understand that God expects the people whom we serve in ministry to support us, but that support must never be manipulated and initiated to favor us beyond reasonability. Every deposit that we make into people must produce a return that favors more than just the depositor. It's easy to teach people that it's better to give than to receive when you are the recipient of that which they give. When I was led, after much prayer 26 years ago, not to take a set salary from my church, but to live on whatever love offering the people gave me, it was a test of my faith. I was asked how I could trust people in that way; my answer to that was simple: I'm not trusting people to do right by me, but I'm trusting God to direct the heart of His people concerning me. I have never lacked for anything since that day unless it occurred by my own financial negligence. Like Joshua, I was instructed to stick to the vision, the Word of God, and to stay the course of focus. As a result, I have won many battles that were set against me, overcome traps that were set to make me stumble, but God has proven himself faithful. He has made my name known among many, has opened many doors in my life, and many doors are yet to be opened. I love leading his people toward their chosen place of destiny; I love feeding His people the words He provides. But I have no need to control them to me, only to carry them toward Him.

Joshua was faithful to that which God instructed of him. He had a few stumbles along the way from within the camp of Israelites, but he stayed submitted to God, even during times of chastisement. His name became favored, feared, and famous during his reign of leadership. He won many great victories and led the children of Israel into the land of promise as promised. Joshua was truly committed to God and had pledged that he and his house would serve the Lord. Joshua died at the age of one hundred and ten. The following words spoke of his life and leadership:

> And Israel served the Lord all the days of Joshua, and all the days of the elders that over-lived Joshua, and which had known all the works of the Lord, that he had done for Israel. — Joshua 24:31

Leading God's people is always about them serving Him faithfully under your leadership, not them serving your vision and cause. If the people you lead can't tell you as much about God as they can about you, then the question becomes how well did you lead them and feed them, or did you just need them for your own purposes? Israel served the Lord all the days of Joshua, not Joshua, and that's the way it should always be.

SAUL

The dynamics surrounding the life and leadership of Saul are tempered and initiated by the rebellious will of the people of Israel to circumvent God's plan to follow the systems of other nations. The people wanted a King system instead of a Judge. They knew that Samuel was getting old, and they didn't trust his sons, who were judges over the people, because they were not following in their father's prophetic footsteps. The prophet Samuel was totally disturbed by this and sought the Lord:

> And Samuel heard all the words of the people, and he rehearsed them in the ears of the Lord. And the Lord said to Samuel, Hearken unto their voice, and make them a king. And Samuel said unto the men of Israel, Go ye every man unto his city. — 1 Samuel 8:21–22

What we learn here is the danger of the people choosing a leader after their own heart as opposed to one chosen after the heart and plan of God. What you will also learn is the manner by which God respects the freedom of will and choice. So even though chapter nine of 1 Samuel proves that God chose Saul, He did so based on the desires of the people's heart for a king. It is interesting to note that when you study proceeding chapters nine through twelve, Saul was doing well in following God and the prophet Samuel. But when you get to chapter thirteen, you see Saul becoming more of a crowd pleaser than a God pleaser. He forgets that every battle he had won was not done on the strength of the people nor his leadership, but on the strength and structure that God had instituted.

This is the perpetual downfall of many pastoral leaders in the Church today; they assume that based on their intellectual prowess, their charismatic gifts, and their popularity with the people frees them to take liberties that are outside of the scope of their assignment and anointing.

This is the perpetual downfall of many pastoral leaders in the Church today; they assume that based on their intellectual prowess, their charismatic gifts, and their popularity with the people frees them to take liberties that are outside of the scope of their assignment and anointing. We must always remember that we are all anointed for specific assignments, not self-selected liberties. I will continue to repeat this throughout this book; these are not our people, and we can't ascribe to their praise of us, or our need for their acceptance. Such actions come with a great price that none of us can afford to pay. Leading and feeding God's people without being swayed by your own inclinations are the mandates for your pastoral assignment.

Samuel's Determined Delay Became Saul's Definite Demise

Take a look at how Saul's leadership took a downward spiral, and how this impacted the future of the Israelite nation and kingdom. Saul was chosen of God, but something happened that was not initiated by God. Saul decided he wanted to please the people and had tried to protect their loyalty to himself, so he tried to operate outside of his anointing, putting his hands into what only the prophet Samuel had the anointing to do.

> And he tarried seven days, according to the set time that Samuel had appointed: but Samuel came not to Gilgal; and the people were scattered from him. And Saul said, Bring hither a burnt offering to me, and peace offerings. And he offered the burnt offering. And it came to pass, that as soon as he had made an end of offering the burnt offering, behold, Samuel came; and Saul went out to meet him, that he might salute him. And Samuel said, What hast thou done? And Saul said, Because I saw that the people were scattered from me, and that thou camest not within the days appointed, and that the Philistines gathered themselves together at Michmash; Therefore said I, The Philistines will come down now upon me to Gilgal, and I have not made supplication unto the Lord: I forced myself therefore, and offered a burnt offering. —1 Samuel 13:8–12

What I am about to discuss next may not sit well with the theological and doctrinal beliefs of many pastors who don't believe in all the ascension gifts, especially the gift or office of the apostle and prophet; however, not many dispute the gift and office of the evangelist, pastor and teacher while some see pastor and teacher as one. But that's another debate for a different book. I believe that all these gifts are essential to the growth maturation of God's people and God's Kingdom Church. The prophetic voice within the Church is necessary, but I don't believe that every pastor is a prophet, and I don't believe that prophets make good pastors—unless they have pastoral grace upon them. Pastors are unique and distinct in their gifting; they have a sensitivity to the sheep, which prophets and apostles do not have. Needless to say, I have been blessed of God to operate in all the gifts of Ephesians 4:11–14:

> And he gave some, apostles; and some, prophets; and some, evangelists; and some, pastors and teachers; For the perfecting of the saints, for the work of the ministry, for the edifying of the body of Christ: Till we all come in the unity of the faith, and of the knowledge of the Son of God, unto a perfect man, unto the measure of the stature of the fulness of Christ: That we henceforth be no more children, tossed to and fro, and carried about with every wind of doctrine, by the sleight of men, and cunning craftiness, whereby they lie in wait to deceive; But speaking the truth in love, may grow up into him in all things, which is the head, even Christ:

But I do differ from the thinking of many that, even though I have all the gifts, I do not believe I should function in all of those offices. I believe that God has placed everything within the Body of Christ to the point of sharing those offices with other people who walk in these apostolic gifts. I have prophets, evangelists, pastors and teachers in my congregation, and I serve as the apostle servant in our church. Saul was king with some prophetic gift, but he was not the assigned prophet and, therefore, should have been offering any sacrifices on behalf of the people. He himself says he did not make supplication to God; in other words, he did not pray for God's direction, but he said he forced himself to do what he did. To force yourself is to engage yourself into something you do not have the power or permission to do. So you know what happened? God did not accept it, and He rejected the sacrifice as well as Saul. Look at what Scripture says:

> And Samuel said to Saul, Thou hast done foolishly: thou hast not kept the commandment of the Lord thy God, which he commanded thee: for now would the Lord have established thy kingdom upon Israel forever. But now thy kingdom shall not continue: the Lord hath sought him a man after his own heart, and the Lord hath commanded him to be captain over his people, because thou hast not kept that which the Lord commanded thee. —1 Samuel 13:13–14

God fired Saul and had already picked his successor, but did not inform Saul of who he was, only that he was. He left Saul on the job but took away his influence by taking his anointing. Whenever leaders choose to follow their own wisdom and ways and the desires of the people, you cease to be effective in God's eyes. He'll let you continue as the hired hand of the people, but your power and ability to impact the kingdom will be removed from you. Even after God left Saul in place, he proved that he could not be trusted and dishonored God in how he handled the events concerning the Amalekites. **Read 1 Samuel chapters 14 and 15.**

> And Saul said unto Samuel, I have sinned: for I have transgressed the commandment of the Lord, and thy words: because I feared the people, and obeyed their voice. Now therefore, I pray thee, pardon my sin, and turn again with me, that I may worship the Lord. And Samuel said unto Saul, I will not return with thee: for thou hast rejected the word of the Lord, and the Lord hath rejected thee from being king over Israel. And as Samuel turned about to go away, he laid hold upon the skirt of his mantle, and it rent. And Samuel said unto him, The Lord hath rent the kingdom of Israel from thee this day, and hath given it to a neighbor of thine, that is better than thou. — 1 Samuel 15:24–28

It is apropos that I expound a little further on this Saul-type leadership. When God assigns us to His people, He does so with the clear intent that we will follow him at all points. So many perverted ideological heresies have arisen within the Church that are not of the Spirit. The parading and invading of humanistic doctrines that serve the belly of men and do nothing to expand people's relationship with God has become more frequent than ever. I have seen it, and I am opposed to it emphatically and am encouraging others not only to take note of it but also to teach and to preach against it. Let me be very clear. This is not a witch hunt against the people who God has called; this is a challenge to get us to refocus our visions and make sure that God remains at the forefront of where we are leading His people. Don't need them, but feed them and lead them into the arms of their creator and savior, right where they belong. Let our desire always remain in pleasing God and staying loyal to His voice, vision and values. So much prosperity and richness of spirit is within Him, so we have no need to bounty for anything from the sheep.

DAVID

It is interesting to see within the biblical narrative of Samuel and Saul that God demoted Saul. And when Samuel spoke to Saul, he said that God had chosen someone who was after his heart.

> But now thy kingdom shall not continue: the Lord hath sought him a man after his own heart, and the Lord hath commanded him to be captain over his people, because thou hast not kept that which the Lord commanded thee. — 1 Samuel 13:14

The anointing has already been assigned to someone else, even though that person has not been notified. God chose David before he ever called him, and now Israel will get the man of God's choice and not the man of its choosing. David was perfect for what God had in mind, even though biblical history shows he did not fit the stature that was within the tradition of men. As a pastor the only qualification is to love God with all of your heart, soul and spirit and be chosen by God. He knows who He wants and what form He wants that person to possess. God is aware of everyone's past, present and future, but He chooses in spite of what He knows about that person, good or bad.

This is what God should get from those whom He calls—servants who are after his heart and not after the heart of the people or any other thing that's not of Him. David was not a perfect man as most of us know, but his heart for God is to be revered, recognized and remembered. That's the source of his worship, his heart for God above all things. David's life has many intervals because he was such a unique leader, filled with passion, wisdom, courage, influence, charisma and character. If favor, prosperity and success are what you are looking for as a God-appointed leader, then keeping your heart pure and pointed toward him will get you there every time. The Bible declares, **"The blessings of the Lord makes a person rich, and he adds no sorrow with it"** Proverbs 10:22, NLT.

I see the pastoral assignment as a blessing, and I took this thinking posture as I began to mature and understand God better, even though I knew

I could know him extensively but not exhaustively. I came to understand that total focus on him and less focus on a need of the people would land me where I was destined and determined by Him to be. I've always wanted success, prosperity and progress, but I preferred that it came from Him and not by my manipulating the people that He appointed me to lead. This must be the foundation of every pastor's motive because tempting challenges will try to persuade you in directions that are motivated by your flesh. Stay with God, stay focused and attentive to Him, and shepherd his sheep accordingly. He will prosper you, but you must never put your needs above the needs of God's sheep. Feed them the Word of God in depth and watch them develop into whom God has purposed them to be. In that, you will find that he will turn their hearts toward you in a way that is not manipulated by you, but mandated by Him.

David served as king over two nations of God's people, even though certain historical events caused his legacy to lose one. However, he was so God forward that never in his heart did he stray from that course. He did do things in following his flesh senses, like sleeping with Bathsheba and having her husband, Uriah, killed to cover his own tracks. He also took a census of his people to determine his ability to win in battle—when every battle he had won was actually because of the power of God. But his heart remained pure for God, even though his flesh got the best of him in those moments. I'm sure every pastor has had some kind of flesh-interrupted moments. David was oftentimes celebrated by the people, but he never became influenced by them or a need for them emotionally or mentally. When his men talked of stoning him in Ziglag (1 Samuel 30:6), he didn't fall under the pressure of concern over where he stood with them; he encouraged himself in the Lord, not in the people. God gave him victory after victory because of how he worshipped and served the Lord. We are called to serve the Lord, even when we are serving His people. When you don't build high expectations of receiving from them, you minimize emotional setbacks and low self-esteem if they don't respond according to your needs. When you look to God for everything that you need as a person and a pastor, you are guaranteed a level of life and style that only He can give you and that which no man can take away.

> **Stay with God, stay focused and attentive to Him, and shepherd his sheep accordingly. He will prosper you, but you must never put your needs above the needs of God's sheep.**

Keep the sheep for God, and him only. Let your life be an example of such. Don't be manipulated by the pressures of what you see other men and women of God do. Much of what we are seeing in the Body of Christ today is not manufactured by the Holy Spirit, but by the appetites of men for fame, fans and fortune. It is embarrassing to the ministry, and it's motivated by a harlot spirit of pay for play, and many are so pridefully arrogant and controlled by a spirit of self-entitlement. I hope and pray that those of you who are reading this information will consider it soberly and not by sarcastic and seditious intoxication. I do not, in any way or form, make any reference to any specific person in this chapter or any other chapter in this book. I stand firmly on the content that is interpreted here and pray that the Body of Christ is being edified by what is written. **Lead them, feed them, but don't need them is not the question, but it is the answer.**

CHAPTER FOUR

BECAUSE YOU CAN, SHOULD YOU?

Knowing right from wrong is a moral necessity in life; choosing which path to follow is totally self-conclusive and self-determined. Individual choices are the patterns that shape the scope of our perceptions and ideologies, and they often expose the levels of our intellectual and spiritual aptitudes. However, those perceptions and ideologies must come under the judicatory scrutiny of biblical, moral and civil rulings. Rights and rules, though they are privileges and freedoms, must be understood as freedoms that do not free you from responsibility, nor do they endorse any forms of ignorance. Wisdom is the ability to properly manage the freedoms and favors we are free to enjoy. Wisdom is a discipline, and discipline is a maturity strategy that is exercised, so we can be our best self at all times, regardless of the freedoms and favors we are given in life. Because you can do something or have something, it doesn't mean you should engage yourself into a particular thing. I was raised under the guidance of a principle of discipline that said everything that's good to you is not always good for you. Another principle said everything you are good at, you shouldn't go at.

Within the context of creditability of character, we have to make some conclusive decisions that will demand of us what I call liberation from certain freedoms. This liberation is not a form of bondage, but a form of best choice, considering what's presently at stake. You should not allow external influences from other sources to bring pressure on you because you must live not for the moment but for the future. Some people make the mistake of putting all their chips on the present, but they put at risk all future opportunities or possibilities. You have to care as much about your future as you do your present. Both future and present may not be roommates, but they do have to ultimately live with each other's consequences, even though they share a geographical divide at the moment. **Your present decides for your future, but your future determines if it can carry you to the next level. But the past will tell the truth about both.**

Now let me take you to where I am going within the context of this book, so you can see how my opening argument is designed to usher you into a line of thinking that is prevalent to the role and responsibility of shepherding sheep. Be mindful that I use metaphorically and interchangeably the terms pastor and shepherd as well as sheep and people throughout this book. The only way for me to remain proof positive in both content and context, I must reference biblical data, not to impose my will upon agnostics or atheistic ideologies or the biblical interpretations of others. But this author believes in God; I am called of God, and I believe his Word as recorded in Scripture and also by the instructed teachings of the Holy Spirit, from whence the Bible is inspired. Side bar reference: Isn't it amazing how the Bible is inspired and unveiled by the Holy Spirit, but when people attempt to fully interpret it and understand it, they go solely on what someone else dictates based on the credibility of their scholastic and academic pedigree? Don't forget that the Holy Ghost is still the agent of checks and balances in God's Word.

Today, some pastors make the mistake of leaving the legacy of their life totally to what they do at church. On so many occasions, after a pastor has passed on, his family is left in struggle and strain and, in some cases, poverty and without the comforts they had become accustomed to.

As we are introduced to a man named Saul in the New Testament's Book of Acts, you will see him, not when he was in his educational and religious training, but when he was in his spiritual transition. We find him in Acts 7:56 as a spectator and solicitor of the persecution of one of the first deacons named Stephen, **"And cast him out of the city, and stoned him: and the witnesses laid down their clothes at a young man's feet, whose name was Saul."**

This young religious radical was against Christianity and the teachings of Christ; he was an agitator and persecutor of the new Christian Reformation. Even though Saul was carrying out a plan that was against God, he was traveling on a path chosen for him by God, and he had no clue. You can read more about his transition in Acts, starting with chapter nine. What I want to point out is what is known of his profession as a tentmaker. Acts 18:3 says, **"And because he was of the same craft, he abode with them, and wrought: for by their occupation they were tentmakers."**

We should note that even though Saul, whose name is now Paul in this reference, was an apostle. He was also an entrepreneur who owned his own business. Paul did not think it was beneath him to take responsibility for his own financial future. He never left his total personal care to the churches he planted and gave oversight to. He remained invested in himself by continuing to use the skills he had in this area of profession. Today, some pastors make the mistake of leaving the legacy of their life totally to what they do at church. On so many occasions, after a pastor has passed on, his family is left in struggle and strain and, in some cases, poverty and without the comforts they had become accustomed to. This happens because another pastor and his or her family has assumed that role and are now getting those benefits. I am totally not against the Church taking care of the men and women of God who watch over it, but I do believe we have to exercise wisdom in how we embrace that care. I'll talk more about excess in a later chapter, but here I want to stay focused on the potential abuse of power based on what you can do as opposed to what you should do.

The Apostle Paul, throughout his ministry, laid many foundations for churches and served as a spiritual father to pastors and their churches. He was responsible for bringing Gentiles into the Apostolic Reformation of the Church, teaching them about Christ, the Holy Spirit, grace, justification, sanctification and many other Christian doctrines. Paul, by right, could have held the churches under his apostleship, totally responsible for their care, but he made his testimony of Christ and the truth of God's Word as the burden on the people. He was never compelled to impose some kind of apostolic taxation upon the people. In Philippians 4:10–19, he writes a letter of commendation and gratitude to the Philippians, but he clearly defines that his focal priority for them was their bearing fruit for Christ.

> But I rejoiced in the Lord greatly, that now at the last your care of me hath flourished again; wherein ye were also careful, but ye lacked opportunity. Not that I speak in respect of want: for I have learned, in whatsoever state I am, therewith to be content. I know both how to be abased, and I know how to abound: everywhere and in all things I am instructed both to be full and to be hungry, both to abound and to suffer need. I can do all things through Christ which strengtheneth me. Notwithstanding ye have well done, that ye did communicate with my affliction. Now ye Philippians know also, that in the beginning of the gospel, when I departed from Macedonia, no church communicated with me as concerning giving and receiving, but ye only. For even in Thessalonica ye sent once and again unto my necessity. Not because I desire a gift: but I desire fruit that may abound to your account. But I have all, and abound: I am full, having received of Epaphroditus the things which were sent from you, an odour of a sweet smell, a sacrifice acceptable, wellpleasing to God. But my God shall supply all your need according to his riches in glory by Christ Jesus. — Philippians 4:10–19

Oftentimes, when this passage is taught, emphasis is made on the people's care for their leaders and God supplying their needs as a result of it. Now that point is true and clear in this text. However, the point that must not be minimized is the manner by which Paul trusted God and suffered willingly, making both mental and physical adjustments in times of lack or need. It is vitally important that pastors understand the ministry of struggle and suffering for righteousness' sake. Many of my charismatic colleagues and friends may differ with me on this matter because many of them tie suffering to a lack of faith. I believe that faith is developed by the Word and through the warfares we face on the human landscape. Paul found himself in some places of lack, but his lack on many occasions was overcome by his faith loyalty, which empowered him to find a containment of comfort within the context of contentment. He also writes in Philippians 1:29, **"For you have been given not only the privilege of trusting in Christ but also the privilege of suffering for him."**

Though Jesus was God's Son, he learned obedience by the things that he suffered; *he experienced them and endured them, he tasted them and triumphed over them,* according to Hebrews 5:8, emphasis added.

Psalm 34:19 is also an echoing voice of the human experience and the experience of those who serve the cause of the Kingdom of God. The Psalmist says, **"Many are the afflictions of the righteous; but the Lord delivereth him out of them all."**

The point I'm making is not just to offer an apologetical defense to the doctrine of suffering, but also to show us that even though Paul had certain privileges, he paused on them at times for the witness of his testimony. He was more interested in God being gloried and Jesus being exalted amongst men, so he put his own prerogatives under his personal discipline. This is the attitude that shapes the foundation of this chapter: the wisdom to say emphatically that even though I can get from these people, by right, financial care, I will not jeopardize the integrity of my pastoral call for tangible belongings. As pastors we have to think outside the box of our own personal need and desire; we are under so much scrutiny by the world due to the greed of many. Those of us who know better must do better to change that suspicious alarm that has become the thinking norm within society at large. Do not allow the spirit of arrogance and entitlement to compel you into thinking that as a pastor you shouldn't worry about what people say. I agree you shouldn't worry about it, but you should consider what they say. Jesus made such an inquiry in Matthew 16:13 when he asked the disciple, **"Who do people say the Son of Man is?"** You can interpret that statement as you choose, but he shows consideration for what the people thought, but he was more concerned about how his inner circle of disciples interpreted his sonship. The Apostle Paul writes:

> **Do not allow the spirit of arrogance and entitlement to compel you into thinking that as a pastor you shouldn't worry about what people say.**

> Let not then your good be evil spoken of: For the kingdom of God is not meat and drink; but righteousness, and peace, and joy in the Holy Ghost. For he that in these things serveth Christ is acceptable to God, and approved of men. Let us therefore follow after the things which make for peace, and things wherewith one may edify another. — Romans 14:16–19

I make no rhetorical assumptions here, so study these Scriptures prayerfully and allow your mind to be pricked to the point of an attentive response. Too much is at stake in the Kingdom of God for us to be putting our own wealth above the furtherance of the gospel. There is nothing wrong with being rich or wealthy, but use your gifts and talents and skills in an entrepreneurial way that separates your financial legacy from your legacy as a pastor. Even though you may deserve to receive double honor, don't be double ignorant and ignore the bigger picture, which is to win souls to the Kingdom of God. The question still remains relevant: What does it profit a man if he gains the whole world but loses his soul? The essence of who we are is not defined by anything material, but spiritual. We must regulate our freedoms and not be so vain in our aspirations. God is never going to allow that those whom He calls be in lack. Whenever your personal agenda as a pastor preempts the agenda of the Kingdom of God and His Church, you are not a true shepherd, but a hireling.

My Personal Testimony

I have been in pastoral ministry as a Senior Pastor for 37 years. For me it has been the most rewarding and refreshing season of my life. I have always approached this role with sincerity and passion. I began my first pastoral assignment in a small church that had never had a full-time pastor, so it didn't offer full-time pay or benefits of any kind. I had promised God that if He assigned me to a church, I would give myself fully to that responsibility. So I quit a very good paying job with lucrative benefits, never imagining the cost and effect it would have on my family and me financially; I just went all the way in. For me it was never and has never been about the money, but the joy of serving God's people. I developed a faith in God for my provisions. And even when the people I pastored didn't meet my needs, God always provided for me, even though things were consistently tight and burdensome. I never complained, neither did I compromise my assignment. Although I faced some hard challenges and was confronted by some negative forces against me, I knew who called me and for whom I worked; it sure wasn't the people who asked for my services. This was my first assignment, and I must admit, it was the hardest decision of my life to leave that church to move to Daytona Beach, Florida, a distant place for what was a better opportunity. The only thing that compelled me to leave was not the increase in pay and finally getting benefits for my family me, but I knew that it was the will of God.

Ultimately, as time passed and God assigned me to Miami to Bethel Baptist Church in Richmond Heights, it was never about the pay, only the promise of God to guide me and my promise to obediently follow Him. Understanding that I had so many other talents within myself, I began to dream about ways to enrich myself as an entrepreneur, so I could give of myself to the ministry of Bethel without having to receive a salary. I discovered during that time that I had a gift of writing, something that I never saw within myself. I also had a passion for cooking and always wanted to own my own restaurants. I always had the gifts of singing, but I discovered that I was a songwriter as well as a producer and director of stage plays and movies. Over the years, I have been able to do all of these things, and I must say all these endeavors proved to be potentials for great success at some point. However, all of these things take up a lot of time and focus, and I've discovered that time given to anything is time away from something else.

Over the past 29 years, Bethel has been very good to me on so many levels—seeing after my family and me as only they would be willing to do. They have been faithful to me, and I have tried to be as faithful to them while we all remained faithful to God. They would give me anything that I asked them for; but more than anything, they gave me the freedom to lead without questions, even when they had valid reasons to be concerned at times. I move very fast and can be a very spontaneous and impulsive leader. I am also not the best communicator; this has been one of my weaknesses. Out of all the freedoms I had and still do have, I had to learn not to abuse those freedoms. And in some cases, I may have abused them but not intentionally. As I begin to see myself in other dimensions of purpose filled life, I recognize that I am in a transition that is moving me away from full-time senior pastor responsibility. I am a world changer, a builder of communities, a reformer against racial injustices, an entrepreneur and philanthropist. A part of my transition is to complete every vision assignment that God gave me for Bethel and to leave it in a state of financial security and freedom from debt, and to engrave into the fabric of the future a structure of order and organization that is second to none in the world. Ultimately, it is my goal to give back to them every financial gift they've ever given to me, before I totally shift into my apostolic role in the world.

I share this with you because I want you to glean from my briefly written biography the importance of not reducing your life or mental state down to your role as pastor. God never intended for you to make His Church your source for financial gain. He said that the money coming in was for meat in His house, not yours. The presumptive attitude has been in many cases that the pastor is supposed to get the bulk of the meat. Under Old Testament law, tithes were used at the discretion of the priest to ensure that the house of God and those who rendered service in the Temple were cared for. Under New Testament grace, many pastors have made themselves the priority of care, not that you shouldn't be a priority. You must be wise and discerning and know that your power to have should not lend itself to a power to always take. Use your other talents to secure yourself financially, not the offerings. It's just not a good look and not an ethical practice to implement. God is your source, so let him be the Lord who makes provisions for you. Don't do things just because you can; do them only if you determine you should in a given situation. Paul lays out a principle to practice in 1 Corinthians 6:12. He boldly speaks of this by saying, **"All things are lawful unto me, but all things are not expedient: all things are lawful for me, but I will not be brought under the power of any."**

The point is clear, yet this Scripture is sometimes misunderstood. Paul is saying that just because something is legally lawful, it doesn't make it spiritually appropriate. If we were to do everything we wanted to do or had the right to do, we would ultimately become a slave to that thing. This is how bondages are formed. They start out being freedoms. Then those freedoms become undisciplined, and now you are enslaved by your flesh, and you end up compromising your whole ministry and reputation. Enticements are ultimate entanglements that cunningly draw you into itself and away from the ways of God. "Just because you can, it doesn't mean you should" is a great principle that should become a mandate in how you govern your path as a pastor.

> "All things are lawful," but not all things are helpful.
> "All things are lawful," but not all things build up. Let no one seek his own good, but the good of his neighbor.
> — 1 Corinthians 10:23–24, ESV

My prayer for you is that you walk in truth and power, overcoming every tempting thing that tries to manipulate your effectiveness by reducing you down to that which only feeds on flesh. Never put the needs of yourself in front of the needs of the people you are called to lead. Make sure also that you heed to this in the context of your being a shepherd. Don't let this statement or any of my statements be an authorization for you to neglect your family. There is so much more to be said, so let's move to the next chapter of challenges and changes that must be met head-on with truth.

CHAPTER FIVE

When Is Enough, Enough?

In the last chapter, I laid out some principles and postures that are designed to help employ wisdom and discipline to the freedoms we have been given. In this chapter, I want to constructively confront the excess and flamboyancy that has found its way aggressively into the Christian Church culture. There appears to be a competitive dual among the charismatic constituency of the clergy to see who can have the biggest and the best, the most and the magnificent. This vain entitlement of material excessiveness has eclipsed the true passion for the work of ministry, causing the focus of many to seek after the potential wealth of ministry. Unfortunately, much of this excess is acquired on the backs of the people who God has called us to feed, not to feed on. In order to have an understanding of what I am saying here, I must tell you what I am not saying. I am not in any way suggesting any opposition to you enjoying and spending your money on things that you enjoy. I'm aware many people like their material trinkets and toys; I have things I enjoy myself. My mother used to tell me the only difference between men and boys are the size of their toys. That is true because the older we get, the bigger and costlier our toys get, and it is then that we have to employ some discipline to our desires. The bottom line truth is I am emphatically not opposed to pastors or Christians obtaining material wealth.

If you have been blessed to accrue financial wealth through smart business dealings, investments and product sales such as your books, music or productions you produce, then good for you. If you want a big house, nice cars and to dress nice, that's good for you. However, I believe it takes many streams of income to have the kind of wealth required for us to enhance the Kingdom of God work. I favor personal entrepreneurship myself and am the owner of many companies I am developing, ultimately, to become resources that will financially sustain my family, me and the philanthropic agenda I have set as a life goal. Now that I am sixty, having been in ministry forty-one years with thirty-seven of those years serving as a Senior Pastor, I am now reducing my pastoral role and beginning to prepare to transition my life and time in a way that will allow me to enrich myself, so I can accomplish my philanthropic goals, which will include enhancing the economic base of many impoverished black communities.

The purpose of this literary conversation is to help us understand that we cannot and should not use the Church as our fishing pools for success.

The purpose of this literary conversation is to help us understand that we cannot and should not use the Church as our fishing pools for success. I'm going to keep saying this throughout this book because the Church doesn't belong to us. We didn't launch it. We didn't give our life for the world, so men can come to us and establish our kingdom. We had no part in its conception. Yes, God did use men as vehicles to birth what He conceived, but we are not the parent. The doctor who delivered your child is not the parent of the child, but the people who contributed the sperm and eggs are. It doesn't matter if you are the founder of a local assembly. Once you call it Church, it comes under the biblical government of God, Jesus and the Holy Spirit who are all one.

I am not saying people should not support us, but I am saying we should not manipulate them for our gain. We are not the glory of the Church, and we should not flaunt ourselves in such pious pretension while lusting for these platforms of praise while placing excessive financial responsibility on the backs of the people. Greed is guaranteed to get you grounded by God, and then you'll know that all your gain was in vain. Aligning riches to Christian righteousness, material prosperity to faith and giving, and if you don't give, you won't prosper are a bit excessive and partly misrepresentations of the Bible's teaching on wealth.

Once you are graced and honored to shepherd God's people, self-sacrificing factors will play into that narrative. You shouldn't bring your personal dreams of prosperity and wealth into the scope of God's vision for His kingdom and His people. You have to keep your personal life interests away from what belongs to God. You have to consider that most of the people we lead may never reach the pinnacles of wealth and success that some of us are favored to reach. Besides, they don't have the network of people at their exposure like many of us do. If they did, they could possibly experience the same. You have to truly be filled with the Spirit and led by the Spirit, so you do not mistake or mislead the sheep and cause them to feel some kind of way when they see you prospering while they are in financial hardship, even some in poverty.

This is not some cloud of confused conjecture coming from a delusional mind. I am speaking truth to power because we are in a serious crisis, and the Church is losing its grip of influence in the world as a result of these kinds of insensitive and inconsiderate behaviors. We must get back to a biblical and spiritual code of ethics that puts a perpetual mandate on our message and our mannerisms. Too many false substitutes are parading themselves as authentic, but they have no witness to substance. Sermonic style and cliches of hyperbole have taken the place of biblical hermeneutics and proper exegesis of the Scriptures. Perspiration-filled sermons have become a replacement for Holy Spirit empowered preaching under the anointing that releases an impartation of revelation power that change the lives of those who are being preached to. This is the new wave, and it is being sold at a high cost because desperate people are vulnerable and, oftentimes, are persuaded and manipulated very easy. As hard and harsh as these things may sound, it is the truth of where we are in the Body of Christ. This is the crisis that has the current generation of millennials straying and staying away from the local church.

We cannot continue on this path we are on, enjoying excessive gain while our people struggle day to day in lack. This is not what Christ had in mind for his people, and it is not the way we see the early Church apostles and leaders conducting themselves. Being extravagant and excessive has its place, but as shepherds of God's people, we must regulate how that extravagance is exemplified by us amongst the people we lead. To me it's a matter of keeping the professional and the personal separate, distinctive and as private as possible. My very close friend Bishop Noel Jones, who happens to be one the most profound homiletic orators of our time, said some very transparent words to me one day. "I am too flawed to be flashy." This conversation occurred behind a comment from someone who was admiring his success and his nice residence, which he acquired through his own personal business acumen, but was surprised at how very casual he was dressed. He further reiterated that just because you have wealth, you don't have to flaunt it, so others can recognize you. I believe that people who respect you solely on what you possess are not true supporters, but fans of your success, not you.

Factors of a Flamboyant and Excessive Lifestyle

When speaking of flamboyancy, I speak of a state of being elaborately or excessively ornamented. This oftentimes comes from a place of feeling the need to be ostentatious. Some people are so insecure within themselves that they tend to exploit certain personal tendencies for the sake of capturing attention. Some people have flamboyant personalities and fashion styles, but that's not what I am referencing here. Flaunting what you have in a braggadocios way and using the pulpit that is designed for preaching to expose it is not appropriate. Allow me to provide you a few of my personal reasons and rationales for coming to this conclusive positioning.

1. It Conveys and Portrays an Image That Is Seen as the Standard for the Christian Lifestyle.

Christian life is never to be perceived as a life without struggle and suffering, but only filled with success and prosperity as the by product. Paul writes in Philippians 1:29 that suffering in behalf of our Christ is a privilege. **"For you have been given not only the privilege of trusting in Christ, but also the privilege of suffering for him"** NLT. Now I understand the difference between suffering for righteousness' sake and suffering because of ungodly choices. Sacrificing your own pleasures for the purposes of a better godly good is to be commended because as pastors, our interest must first be for the good of the people that we lead. If we study the Bible and follow its directives, we would know no Scripture tells us to make riches and wealth our pursuit. We are instructed to pursue the kingdom and its righteous standards and as a result, the things we need will be added unto us. According to Joshua 1:8, when we observe to do all that God requires of us when we have been given an assignment, and we don't go down the path of compromise, prosperity and good success will be an automatic result.

When you promote your excessive lust for things while adding flamboyance and flaunting to it, you are influencing people down a path that says the more you have, the more you are living the kingdom life. The kingdom life is not in the possession of things, but a passion that longs to lay hold onto the things of God. So many teachers have bent the prosperity message way out of theological form and its ideology. I believe that money and wealth are needed in order to advance the Kingdom of God because not only is ministry very extensive and expansive, but it is also very expensive. But when you go to great measures to exploit your possessions—money, cars, houses, planes and status—you are creating an unhealthy church environment. You also open yourself up to unnecessary scrutiny from the world that you are suppose to be influencing toward God. People pay more attention to what we do more than what we say, and what we have more than what we give. Why not tone it down for the sake of the message of the Kingdom of God? You can still enjoy your toys without flaunting them, especially if you didn't get them through ungodly gain. These things draw too much distraction attraction toward us, and it clouds people's ability to see God. Get yourself out of the way!

> **When you promote your excessive lust for things while adding flamboyance and flaunting to it, you are influencing people down a path that says the more you have, the more you are living the kingdom life.**

2. IF YOU DON'T CAREFULLY CURB YOUR APPETITE, YOUR EXCESSIVE BEHAVIORS WILL BE PERCEIVED AS GREED.

> An appetite for good brings much satisfaction, but the belly of the wicked always wants more. — Proverbs 13:25, MSG

The burden of avoiding a possible misconception of ideological views by the people is always on the shoulders of the leader of the people. When we allow our message, methods and motives to go unexplained, it can lead to mangled misinterpretations. Being excessive and flamboyant with material things as a pastor whose only occupation is that of shepherding sheep will make you a suspect, and that should cause you to discipline how you portray yourself. Never be a pastor who lusts and longs for the things of this world at the expense of your testimony; you are called of God, and you must show humility at all times. Some pastors live for the glory of the world when, in fact, God called you to portray that which is a reflection of His character. The pressure to be impressive runs high through the ecclesiastical community, but it's a false pressure designed by the enemy to draw on your affections and not your assignment. Your true taste will be tested in time, and your motives will be unveiled not only to you but to others. In order to pass the taste tests, which come to show you your own authentic allegiances to the call, you must maintain a healthy ear to the voice of the Spirit. The Holy Spirit won't let you stray nor self-destruct as long as your heart is pure toward him and not some need for greed.

> **Never be a pastor who lusts and longs for the things of this world at the expense of your testimony; you are called of God, and you must show humility at all times.**

When you put so much emphasis on material things and display an appetite for fame and fortune in excess, you can be perceived as being guilty of filthy lucre. If everything you say and do as a pastor is always centered in financial positioning and prospering, then that can arouse a suspicion amongst the sheep that borderlines greed. As a leader of God's people, success and prosperity are certainties if you follow the biblical blueprint without compromise. What you must not do is allow an unhealthy desire for success to manipulate and control your own human and fleshly propensities. Your flesh will never be born again. You have to intentionally put your flesh to death—if not, it will kill your power and influence. It's within human nature to desire the things of the flesh, and the flesh is never satisfied no matter how much you feed it; it always wants more. If you do not have your priorities in check and understand that the profit of material things has no eternal value, you will make a mockery of yourself and the ministry.

> For what doth it profit a man, to gain the whole world,
> and forfeit his life? — Mark 8:36, ASV

There was a time in my life as a pastor when I felt the pressure of the international speaking platform I was on. I felt this need to fit into a category of preachers who were boastful of how much they had, how big their congregations were, how big there house was, and how many cars they drove. You can lose yourself and your focus if you're not careful to have restraints and focus on why God called you in the first place. Our success in ministry and the financial gain we see come into our ministries are not for us to have free control of and total access to. Of course, we should reap when we sow and where we sow, but don't monopolize the harvest for yourself. Money and wealth can satisfy only a certain small dimension of your life, but it can never fulfill all of it, so don't be deceived by it. Listen to the teaching of Jesus as recorded by the gospel writer Mark.

> And the cares of this world, and the deceitfulness of
> riches, and the lusts of other things entering in, choke
> the word, and it becometh unfruitful. — Mark 6:19,
> KJV

Your life and your ministry are and should be more about spiritual reproduction than it is about financial reciprocity. Nothing should be as important to you as the effectiveness of the Word of God. Mismanagement of your flesh can make your preaching of no effect. What you make happen to advance the Kingdom of God is so much more important than what you reap from the Kingdom of God. The royalties that will come from an obedient life to God can never be calculated at a bank, measured by square footage, or defined by a car's beauty or engine horsepower. Put some discipline to your materialistic diet before you become overweighted with a greed that you'll never be able to satisfactorily feed.

3. BE CONSIDERATE WHEN REFERENCING YOUR ACCUMULATION OF MATERIAL POSSESSIONS; YOU HAVE MORE LISTENERS WITHOUT IT THAN WITH IT.

The Spirit has aligned my attention most specifically to the financial lack of so many people who occupy the seats in local churches week after week. These people are loyal attendees who attend consistently and give of their resources faithfully, only to be taught in many cases, manipulated motivational messages that inspire them, but don't increase them. Then you have the audacious preacher who brags about what God is doing for him or her, but the evidence is not seen at levels that would prove the principles preached are working for the people who are listening. Over the years, I've heard preachers say about such scenarios that "the people have to apply these principles of faith just like we do." Not so and definitely the wrong answer and the wrong attitude. When these messages are spoken to groups of people who are giving to us, we experience financial blessings, but not because we have so much faith, but because we have so many people supporting us financially who believe in us.

Now remember I'm talking strictly about financial prosperity. I am confident there are other areas that when the Word of God is implemented, growth happens for the responders. Now these are hard truths to hear, but it's easy for me to say because the Body of Christ is fractured, and it needs to be fixed. I'll talk more about this in later chapters, but I wanted to inject this thought here, so pastors will be more sensitive and attentive to the needs of their people, considering how much they sacrifice, so we are provided for.

> **Nothing should be as important to you as the effectiveness of the Word of God. Mismanagement of your flesh can make your preaching of no effect. What you make happen to advance the Kingdom of God is so much more important than what you reap from the Kingdom of God.**

Don't stand up week after week using every opportunity to reference what you have, what you bought for your family, and bragging about your lavish vacations. Don't you know many people can't afford a vacation filled with lavish things, but who contribute to your ability to experience what many of them never will? Considering where your people are must never be measured by where you are; assuming something about your people is never a good method—talk with them about where they are and position yourself to lead them into greener pastures. This is the nature of the call of the shepherd, and you should be willing to lovingly understand and stand under them as they strive to live their best life for God and themselves. When you study the life of the apostles and those who were assigned as elders or pastors, you only hear them boasting of spiritual things, not material things. Let this be your example and don't flaunt expressions or actions of how much you have. Following are a few Scriptures that speak to the principle of boasting, which can be applied to this line of thought.

> As it is, you boast in your arrogance. All such boasting is evil. So whoever knows the right thing to do and fails to do it, for him it is sin. — James 4:16–17, ESV
>
> Oh, don't worry; we wouldn't dare say that we are as wonderful as these other men who tell you how important they are! But they are only comparing themselves with each other, using themselves as the standard of measurement. How ignorant! We will not boast about things done outside our area of authority. We will boast only about what has happened within the boundaries of the work God has given us, which includes our working with you. We are not reaching beyond these boundaries when we claim authority over you, as if we had never visited you. For we were the first to travel all the way to Corinth with the Good News of Christ. Nor do we boast and claim credit for the work someone else has done. Instead, we hope that your faith will grow so that the boundaries of our work among you will be extended. Then we will be able to go and preach the Good News in other places far beyond you, where no one else is working. Then there will be no question of our boasting about work done in someone else's territory. As the Scriptures say, "If you want to boast, boast only about the LORD." When people commend themselves, it doesn't count for much. The important thing is for the Lord to commend them." — 2 Corinthians 10:12–18, NLT

There is a line of discipline that has to be drawn, and there must be a resistance against your personal defiance—all because your flesh wants more. No matter how much stuff you get, it will never increase the value of who you are—that within itself, it proves that the push for more isn't worth it. King Solomon in his wisdom gives to us a great perspective regarding wealth. These are Scriptures that you hardly ever hear being taught. It is the aim of this book not to give a shallow rendition of the Scriptures by cherry picking though the Bible and avoiding hermeneutical integrity. I am not trying to prove my point as much as I am trying to convey the whole truth and nothing but the truth as it relates to wealth and prosperity. The love of money is the root of all evil, and many people in the Body of Christ are willing to commit sin in order to enrich their personal coffers.

> "Don't be surprised if you see a poor person being oppressed by the powerful and if justice is being miscarried throughout the land. For every official is under orders from higher up, and matters of justice get lost in red tape and bureaucracy. Even the king milks the land for his own profit! Those who love money will never have enough. How meaningless to think that wealth brings true happiness! The more you have, the more people come to help you spend it. So what good is wealth—except perhaps to watch it slip through your fingers! People who work hard sleep well, whether they eat little or much. But the rich seldom get a good night's sleep."
>
> "There is another serious problem I have seen under the sun. Hoarding riches harms the saver. Money is put into risky investments that turn sour, and everything is lost. In the end, there is nothing left to pass on to one's children. We all come to the end of our lives as naked and empty-handed as on the day we were born. We can't take our riches with us. And this, too, is a very serious problem. People leave this world no better off than when they came. All their hard work is for nothing—like working for the wind. Throughout their lives, they live under a cloud—frustrated, discouraged, and angry. Even so, I have noticed one thing, at least, that is good. It is good for people to eat, drink, and enjoy their work under the sun during the short life God has given them, and to accept their lot in life. And it is a good thing to receive wealth from God and the good health to enjoy it. To enjoy your work and accept your lot in life—this is indeed a gift from God. God keeps such people so busy enjoying life that they take no time to brood over the past." — Ecclesiastes 5:8–20, NLT

So to answer briefly the question of when is enough, enough, I will say it like this. Enough is enough when what you take leaves no room to meet the mandates of the ministry. Enough is enough when you have more in waste and excess than the poor sheep that you lead are living without.

Enough is enough when you feel the Holy Spirit convicting you in this area, but you put it off as if it were the voice of the enemy. Don't allow your pride and potential entitlement to manipulate you into a place of greed. Seek the Lord, even as it relates to this question of thought regarding where you should draw the line on what you take financially from a church. Remember that as shepherds, we work for Jehovah God. He alone should be our voice of reason, not our own psychological prowess. Be prayerful, be careful, and don't let what you see other men and women of God do influence your judgment. I pray that this chapter has offered insights and truths that will cause those of you who find yourselves in these situations to make the right decisions.

CHAPTER SIX

THE SILENCE OF THE LAMB

I have discovered as a head of church that the silence of people under your leadership guidance is not a signal that they are all in favor or in flow with the decisions you are making as their principal. Just because people are not talking to you, it doesn't mean they are not talking to someone else. Ignoring the silence and giving attention only to the applause is a dangerous form of leadership style and can make people feel excluded. It is vital to give audience to the people who don't agree with you as much as it is to give audience to those who do agree with you. Oftentimes, as pastors we see disagreement as a negative, but it is also a positive because it is then that you have the opportunity to win those persons who care about you, but who may not understand what's being asked of them. The fact that these people don't publicly revolt against you, but still show up as a form of support, is a great sign that they do care about you. Now, granted, some people are on the wrong side of truth and good will, but I am not referencing that carnal crowd. Helping people to reach a place of understanding within your ministry will build some very healthy alliances you will need throughout the tenure of your ministry.

I have also discovered as a leader that God gives to pastors everything they need to do the job He has called them to do; and everything that's not there will be there at the appropriate time as the Holy Spirit directs. When Moses was assigned by God to build the tabernacle, he had every resource and skillful person within the camp of the children of Israel. As a result, when Moses called for a collection of finance and material resources from the children of Israel, everything was provided and the outcome was astonishing. The people brought so much material and other needed resources that Moses had to stop them from bringing anything else.

> And they spake unto Moses, saying, The people bring much more than enough for the service of the work which Jehovah commanded to make. And Moses gave commandment, and they caused it to be proclaimed throughout the camp, saying, Let neither man nor woman make any more work for the offering of the sanctuary. So the people were restrained from bringing. For the stuff they had was sufficient for all the work to make it, and too much. — Exodus 36:5–7, ASV

On the strength of the above truth, you must hold to value the people that you are leading. **Just because you are a leader doesn't mean you don't have to listen.** We have what we need in our congregations to do what God requires of us. We don't have to hustle or worry or try and make things happen—just tap into what God has already given you. Now let's talk about the principles of listening.

Listening is an important leadership tool because it helps you to properly govern and discern.

Listening is an important leadership tool because it helps you to properly govern and discern. I want to help those of you who need it in this area not to simplify this reference of thinking. You are a gift from God to the sheep and as much as they should value you, you should also value them and welcome their input. While under the anointing of the Spirit during this writing, I began to be enlightened with a principle I labeled The Strength of Silence. Experience this revelation with me, and please consider it in any area of your life where it can empower you for a better understanding as a leader of God's people.

THE STRENGTH OF SILENCE

Silence is a tactical, intellectual strength that manages its emotions through internal implosions rather than erratic external explosions. It is designed to save strength for the battle and not waste it on the fight; this provides one with the ability to finish strong by reserving both mental and emotional strength to go the distance. The ultimate resolve of every confronting conflict is to get the victory and not just to have a voice. My oldest brother, Ricardo, made this quote when referencing someone who was opposing a certain ideology. He said, "Some people don't want answers; they just want arguments." Silence does not signify simplified stupidity, but sometimes it means a strategy in process. Silence doesn't mean satisfaction in a situation. Sometimes, it means partial settling for the sake of personal and peaceful sanity.

Whenever you silence the voice of the sheep through intentional mental manipulations of intimidation, you silence and sidestep the value of their competence by assuming they are incompetent. Assuming and appealing to the incompetence of people is absolutely assaulting and insulting because it implies you are weakening them to your advantage instead of awakening their inner strength and intellectual potential. I'll say this again, sheep aren't stupid by nature; they are submissive and steady in character. Don't ever assume they don't pay attention and are incapable of raising the volume on their voices. Jesus is called the Lamb of God, not suggesting any forms of weakness, but rather his willful submissiveness to the plans of his Father for his life. When Jesus went into the synagogue and opened the book and began to read, he read from Isaiah 53:7. Luke writes of this account:

> The place of the scripture which he read was this, He was led as a sheep to the slaughter; and like a lamb dumb before his shearer, so opened he not his mouth:
> — Acts 8:32, KJV

Notice the word *dumb* in the text. That word does not mean a form of illiteracy; it means to be silent. In keeping with the theme and title of this chapter, The Silence of The Lamb, I want to continue to advocate against a form or style of leadership that intentionally maneuvers to silence the voice of the sheep. They do have a voice and should be heard as long as they are seeking to know and understand, not just to make negative noise in order to undermine the vision. As a pastor, you are not responsible for making them or forcing them to understand, but you are responsible for helping them to understand. I was watching the news one day, and the media outlet was covering several town hall meetings being held by certain congressional leaders with their constituents. In a particular town hall meeting, the congressman was asked a question by one of his constituents who happened to be an older person. The congressman told that person to shut up! That statement got him much criticism, and he jeopardized his congressional integrity because he acted as if it was beneath him to be asked tough questions that demanded an explanation. Silencing people who oppose your view is not healthy for how you are viewed because opposition against something good will prove the power of that thing. If opposition can weaken it, then it may not have been a great view or idea. Sometimes, opposition can even force you to look deeper and think deeper into the thing you are advocating.

To further perpetuate my line of thinking on this matter, I want to address some things that may not be in your best interest as a servant leader of God's people. These are hard lessons for some of us for a number of reasons, some being a form of insecurity. I have to confess that these things that I share are life lessons for me, even until this very moment. Some of our behaviors are attributed to our personality type, which makes it difficult to break or bend. However, when you are called to a certain level of leadership, you must not allow your distinctive personality to interfere with you performing your duty as a leader of God's people.

Avoiding Communication

Communication is the means by which information is exchanged between individuals through various mediums: verbal (oral and written), symbols, audio and video. Its purpose is for understanding, agreement and to be certain that what has been exchanged has been correctly comprehended. I had to learn and, unfortunately, am still having to force myself to be mindful that just because I spoke it doesn't mean my audience grasped it. Communication is never effective between two or more persons unless a conversation and discussion is taking place on both sides. My problem with communication was the idea of possible confrontation that is sometimes necessary to get everyone on the same page. I always saw confrontation over an issue that I felt was good for the people as their rejection of the vision and me. You can solve more problems and experience sensible solutions by hearing people out. Avoiding effective communication with people over issues that you want them to do can come off as though you are a dictator. It can appear that what you are saying to the people is that you see their value to you only in terms of them doing what you say and not your interest in who they are and what they have to offer. The real problem behind many of the great visions and ideas not coming to pass in our ministries is due to the lack of communication that is the brainchild to execution. People cannot execute properly and appropriately what you don't communicate thoroughly.

Another side to this communication complexity is the fact that we are living in a time when some pastors have risen above the idea of just talking to their people. They come into church and rush out without their sheep having the opportunity to touch or talk to them at any time. I understand the challenge of pastoring a large number of people—been there, done that. But that's not a good reason. It is to be understood that when you have several thousand people in your congregation on a Sunday, you can in no way get to all of those people. However, let your persona be a visual demonstration that you are talkative and touchable. Don't have security people around you giving off gestures that suggest don't touch him or her. Touch and greet as many people as you can with the understanding that you can't talk to all of them. Look at it like this—if all of them had $1,000 each to put into your hands, then you would touch all of them. Again, I know you can't get to all them, and they know that, but greet as many as you can on your way out. But for God's sake, don't push them away nor build a wall with security whose egos are protecting your ego. This is a tough issue to talk about, but I am attempting to speak for the people who don't have the voice to speak for themselves. I am speaking as a pastor who has been guilty of communication challenges, but I've never had an issue with God's people touching or talking to me.

> **Communication is never effective between two or more persons unless a conversation and discussion is taking place on both sides.**

Refusing Accountability

Accountability is a procedural process that says you did what you said you were going to do without compromise or contradiction. It is submitting yourself to other individuals for the purpose of checks and balance. It is a good thing for every pastor to have accountability partners who they respect and expect to give them constructive criticisms. We will get into this topic deeply in chapter ten of this book, where I address and answer the question, "Who's Covering You?" However, I needed to address this issue here because many pastors feel they are above being held accountable by their constituency as it relates to their recourses of actions. The sheep we lead and feed may not say it, but they want us to be held accountable to God. They also want us to be accountable to the earthly sources who provide wise counsel to us as shepherds. Accountability is an act of integrity on behalf of the person who subjects himself to it; it shows great leadership character and strength. Being accountable is not in any way a form of weakness, but it says you trust the power of the vision or goals you are led of God to set. It also reaffirms the trust of the people who are following your leadership.

Stubborn will is an interference of adverse contradiction to accountability; stubborn people care about doing what they want and, at times, never considering the voices of others who may impart something positive to the overall objective. Pastors in some cases do not trust the very people whom they give responsibilities to. This happens when the vision becomes over-protected by the shepherd, and the people aren't allowed the freedom to give ideas to the vision, so it can come to pass. When you have this paranoid need of control, it suggests that maybe you are hiding something for your own protection. I've had to learn this on so many levels of my life, and I can truly say that had I done a better job at inclusion and not fearing the potential rejection of what I believed to be the right decisions, I'd been an even better leader. Even though I must admit that, the people at The Bethel Church have supported me tremendously, even when my decisions were risky and costly. Every pastor is not fortunate to have that kind of support, but I did. Sometimes, things get lonely when you know that what you planned didn't go well, and you avoided input from others. When you have sources you are accountable to, you very wisely have put yourself in protective custody against yourself and/or against any other thing that may lead you down the road of ill-advised decisions. You are responsible for taking as many precautionary measures as you can to show your transparency to the people you lead.

Abuse Of Authority

Abuse of authority is the misuse of authority; it is using the power of your position of influence for personal and profitable gain. Having authority in itself can be very tempting to the people to whom it is given; therefore, it is important to have the right discipline and direction of heart for the people and the work you have been called to do. People in the church trust you to lead them, not to mislead them. And they should not have to be abused by someone who does not know how to handle his or her authority. People with uncertainties about themselves have the tendency to overplay their authority as well as people who are intimidated by others who appear to have an intellectual edge over them. The purpose of having strong, skilled and exceptional people around you within your congregation is not for you to be intimidated by them or for them to be intimidated by you. It is for the purpose of using the best capable people to carry out the vision and mission of the church, so the best results can be accomplished.

Some pastors, unfortunately, use their authority to overshadow or undermine the growth, success and influence that other people have within the church. This happens when pastors see themselves as the most significant gift in the church and the most influential. This in itself is a spirit of conceited humanism and self-deceived dysfunction. Within the Church, the only supreme person of influence should be Christ, working in all believers through the person and power of the Holy Spirit. Pastors should be functioning under divine influence more so than their own strategic or self-manufactured influence. This spirit of exceptionalism has found a place within the hearts of many leaders who believe themselves to be more than they should. Many arrive at this place because they become impressed with themselves while failing to see that God is using other people around them to perpetuate their success. The authority that pastors are given is a delegation of authority from God who is in control of all things. Men ought not overplay their hands of authority, especially allowing it to become tools of abuse that lead them into developing foolish behaviors.

Some pastors even use their knowledge of the Bible abusively for the purpose of control over people within their congregations. This is definitely not a sign of a spiritually mature leader, but rather an immature leader who is not being led of the Holy Spirit, but of his or her flesh. If you are a pastor, then you have been given the Word of God to educate, edify and enlighten your followers of the ways of God. Do not manipulate or emasculate the power and potency of the Word for the purpose of establishing control over people who look for you to present pure truth to them from God. Speaking without biblical text and out of biblical context when leading and teaching God's people is out of bounds and grounds for serious penalty. The irony in all of this is that the sheep are studying the Word more and are biblically well-informed than many people realize. The new Church age of millennials are not easily manipulated or silenced; they ask questions, but they also seek answers themselves, especially if they feel that what they are being told doesn't make sense.

Abuse of authority is totally antithetical to the teachings and instructions of the Bible. If it is not checked, challenged and changed, it opens the door to an occultism spirit, which opens other demonic portals that invite other seducing spirits to enter into the Church. God has set forth in His Word the measure and manner by which He wants his people governed and led. As pastors, we must be held accountable to being spiritually and mentally sane in the management of God's sheepfold. Do not throw your weight around as a pastor, intimidating people just so you can perpetuate an agenda that is not God's. If it were God's agenda, you would have no need to manipulate it. Here are a couple of Scriptures that speaks to the abuse of authority.

> The diseased have ye not strengthened, neither have ye healed that which was sick, neither have ye bound up that which was broken, neither have ye brought again that which was driven away, neither have ye sought that which was lost; but with force and with cruelty have ye ruled them. — Ezekiel 34:4, KJV

> So I exhort the elders among you, as a fellow elder and a witness of the sufferings of Christ, as well as a partaker in the glory that is going to be revealed: shepherd the flock of God that is among you, exercising oversight, not under compulsion, but willingly, as God would have you; not for shameful gain, but eagerly; not domineering over those in your charge, but being examples to the flock. And when the chief Shepherd appears, you will receive the unfading crown of glory. Likewise, you who are younger, be subject to the elders. Clothe yourselves, all of you, with humility toward one another, for "God opposes the proud but gives grace to the humble."
> — 1 Peter 5:1–5, ESV

I hope that the point I make about silencing the sheep has provoked some serious change where it is needed. God's people are a blessing to have walking with you through the many turns within ministry. Don't shut them out or shut them down; bring them in and raise them up to be mature followers of Jesus Christ. You have more to lose as a pastor when you are led by some perverted reason to misuse the people that you're called and sent to serve for their developmental good.

May God do a greater work through his people as both shepherd and sheep work as co-laborers together with God through Christ Jesus. May there be no carnality of competitive clashing that only creates confusion and divisiveness within the Body of Christ. God is glorified whenever His people are unified!

CHAPTER SEVEN

IS ANYBODY LISTENING? THE CRY OF THE SHEEP

> Those who shut their ears to the cries of the poor will be ignored in their own time of need. — Proverbs 21:13, NLT

I chose this Scripture prayerfully because of the profound principles of contextual wisdom and warning that are admonished within its biblical content. Here, the words *poor* and *sheep* are not being misused, but rather they are interchangeable because they relate to exegetical integrity. It is my understanding of the usage of the word *poor* throughout the Scriptures that allows me to exercise ecclesiastical freedom to give illumination and revelation to show the correlation of the word usage to this chapter's content. When the Bible speaks of the poor, it is not always talking about those who have no money or other material resources to meet their human need for the sake of survival. When speaking of the poor, the Bible also talks about *poor in spirit*, which is referencing those who have spiritual deficiencies but acknowledge their need of God in their lives. It is the humility of heart that causes one to expose the truth that money can't solve every human need; some human needs are more spiritual than material. When I think of God's sheep, I also think of their vulnerability and, at times, their undervalued appraisal by those who lead them with unjustifiable recklessness.

The word *sheep* in scriptural presentation is used as a figurative metaphor to give understanding to the gentleness and humble nature that the sheep of God are to portray and or become. It is with this understanding that this chapter takes its form and unfolds truths to be considered and failures to be forgiven. We are to understand that God is very sensitive to the cry of his people and will tolerate their cry until the lessons that He intends for them to learn have been accomplished. When you study the Old Testament narratives regarding the historical afflictions of slavery that were brutally inflicted upon the children of Israel, you will see this principle in motion and in sovereign significance. Observe the Scripture that follows:

> And the Lord said, "I have surely seen the affliction of my people which are in Egypt, and have heard their cry by reason of their taskmasters; for I know their sorrows; And I am come down to deliver them out of the hand of the Egyptians, and to bring them up out of that land unto a good land and a large, unto a land flowing with milk and honey; unto the place of the Canaanites, and the Hittites, and the Amorites, and the Perizzites, and the Hivites, and the Jebusites. Now therefore, behold, the cry of the children of Israel is come unto me: and I have also seen the oppression wherewith the Egyptians oppress them. Come now therefore, and I will send thee unto Pharaoh, that thou mayest bring forth my people the children of Israel out of Egypt." — Exodus 3:7–10, KJV

The operative words of the text are, "I have seen," "I have heard," and "I am come down to deliver them." Notice the grammatical movement of the text and the verbal transitioning of these words. I have seen, past tense; I have heard, past tense; I am come down, present active tense. Here is the essence of what God is saying: He's been seeing them, and He's been hearing them. The whole time that they were experiencing their affliction, He was well aware of their conflict, but He had chosen a set time and a set leader to deliver them out of it. Here's a sovereign principle to learn about God. Whenever He chooses to do or allow a thing, He doesn't have to change it just because it makes some people uncomfortable. Our challenges don't change God, but they are designed to change the person or thing that He is challenging. How long were we thinking that the abuse of God's people—whom he put in the hands of men and, in some cases, women to do what was right by them—would last? Suffering sheep are never forever ignored by God. He chooses a set time and set leaders who are sensitive in heart and submissive in obedience to bring an end to the cries of His people that go unheard in the earth realm. People have endured so much pain within organized religious institutions. This pain is not always self-inflicted or sheep initiated. Sometimes, this abuse comes from the place of pastoral leadership that lacks integrity and sensitivity to those who try to give honest support. The arrogant audacity of men in the pulpit has become an atrocious aching in the heart of God and in Christendom.

> **The arrogant audacity of men in the pulpit has become an atrocious aching in the heart of God and in Christendom.**

So many scandals over the last four decades have been publicly reported but have not been publicly reconciled. When people see that we pastors don't speak out, they are left to assume we are either cowards or cohorts in these scandalous behaviors. I am a believer that all things, regardless of the gravity of the situation, have to be dealt with according to the teachings of the Scriptures. Even though some of these incidents are made public in the media, they do not always have to be played out in the media. However, some kind of public statement should be made to explain the process or explain an opinion or position on the situation. This may not be as simple as I'm making it sound because many churches are independent and not a part of an organized religious reformation in which accountability is enforced. In the epilogue of this book, I share with you my plan to help create resolutions and positive recourses that I believe can be an enhancement in bringing conclusion to this confusion. We have to do more than critique and criticize the problems; we must provide a panacea of improvements for these problems. Let's get busy promoting constructive change instead of being busy bodies promoting destructive criticisms.

THE CRY OF THE INNOCENT

A massive number of people worldwide believe in God and the ministry and message of His kingdom's vision, view and values. This remnant of people are loyal to the core and have not allowed their faith to be shattered by the moral missteps and misbehaving of the men and women of God who have fallen and are held captive to the tendencies and proclivities of their flesh. But yet they cry without complaining because they understand that God will hear them and will bring resolve to the hurt they carry for the Body of Christ. Yes, there are critics who use these negative and vulnerable moments to align themselves to an argumentative agenda that is not in search of answers. But the innocent who also have personal pending flaws in their character choose to cry in intercession to God with the faith that He will fix it. I believe in the restoring power of God and my hope in the Church has not wavered. I believe that the cry of the innocent has been heard and when God is ready, we will see the uprising of true voices for the Kingdom of God. These will be voices that are totally in it for the good of the people and not the gain for themselves. May God, through the Holy Spirit, keep the fire of hope burning and the cry of the innocent bellowing before His face and ears. I am one of many who have heard these cries, seen the afflictions, and have chosen to be used of God to pen this controversial book to bring awareness and answers that will challenge us to a positive response.

THE CRY OF THE INCOMPETENT

Incompetency is defined as the lack of ability to do something accurately not due to intentional ignorance but due to a lack of understanding. I have seen this as a parent, raising children and having to rescue them from their crying tantrums due to their inability to do a particular thing. They put energy and effort into it, but due to their lack of understanding, they surrendered to their frustration instead of seeking knowledge from someone who knew how to make that thing work for them. This is often the response of spiritually immature people who do not understand how things work in the Kingdom of God system. The Word of God is the governing authority for the Body of Christ, not man-made rules or religious emotional antics that attempt to circumvent the Word of God to reach their conclusions on conflicting matters that occur within the family of God. When people don't know better, they can't do better. As a result, they tend to live life cluelessly and aimlessly, not being aware that there is a solution. It is important that we pastors not assume that people truly know how to properly address their concerns to us. When there is no need for a coverup to protect an evil scheme, we as pastors should be willing to give insightful instructions that will remove the frustration from those who have grown weary.

As a pastor, achieving my main goal has never been numerical growth, but the spiritual and intellectual growth that increases the biblical competency level of the people who I am called to lead. Teaching biblical truths will empower people to walk in knowledge and erase their fear of the unknown. When I hear men and women of God fumble through the Bible, committing biblical perjury as they manipulate the minds of people for their own personal gain, I am abhorred. When people are led into and left with an incompetent mind, their cry for understanding can be perceived as complaining due to disagreement. People have to be taught to follow, not just told to follow, especially when they don't have a clue about where they are being taken. When the cry of the incompetent goes unheard, it is not a reflection on the sheep. It is a referendum on the shepherd who is showing poor responsibility as a leader. Pastors, grow your people in the Word of God; don't just groom them to your agendas. Help them to hear, see and understand. You'll gain so much more by doing so, and you will keep your integrity and character as a shepherd in the process.

The Complaint of the Improper

There is a truth to be understood regarding the integral credibility of the majority of the clergy: All pastors are not crooked or wicked, with far more good ones than bad ones. However, some people in their disapprovals are not crying over injustices, but complaining over their improper prejudices and partialities. Improper behavior is manifested on the grounds of lack of facts, truths, and procedures that are out of bounds as they relate to biblical correction or objection. The order of a thing is the integrity of it. And when order is circumvented to cater only to some fleshly disgruntlement, positive production is minimized and maximum confusion is amplified. There has to be a balance of understanding in communication when it comes to complaints regarding a pastor or anyone else. Some people feed off rumors and innuendoes, which are, in essence, oblique allusions of some person's perverted mind. When this happens—and it does happen—people's reputations are damaged, and they end up facing unnecessary scrutiny of character. Pastors are human; we do make mistakes. But many times we do not get a fair hearing in the public system of criticism and judgment. If you don't know a thing to be truth, and you speak out from an improper assessment or judgment, then you lied.

When the Apostle Paul was addressing personal issues of sin at the Church in Corinth, as well as the effectiveness and authenticity of his apostleship, he said, **"This is the third time I am coming to you. In the mouth of two or three witnesses shall every word be established"** 2 Corinthians 13:1. Paul did not play to rumors or uncertainties. He did not just deal in facts. He dealt in truth. The principle here is one to be considered in every area in which the proof of a thing is needed. Don't just run with gossip, seek the gospel truth, the whole truth, and nothing else but the truth. Everything that looks like something is not always the something that it looks like. Improper people in the Church and in the world love controversy and confusion. That is a sign of emotional instability and heightened immaturity. Don't be improper in your judgment of people. As a matter of truth, why not free yourself from judging something until you have all the accurate information regarding that something or individual.

As I write this chapter, headline news is reporting that world renown golfer Tiger Woods was arrested on charges of DUI. Everyone who has given commentary on his situation has declared that he was driving drunk. Even people in the sports world who should know better have already cast him off into oblivion. The truth is he was not drunk; he fell asleep behind the wheel after taking the pain medication Vicodin, which caused him to experience the common side effect of drowsiness. He was on this medication because of recent back surgery, and he didn't use wisdom after taking them. I thank God that he did not injure anyone, including himself. But the judgment went out before evidence had been presented. This happens to people in the spotlight all the time, and some people wait in hate to attack someone's reputation without cause. When I see this in the Church, it is disturbing to me. But I know from experience that even in the Church, there are improper people with improper motives. We must live with all kinds of people, but everyone crying hurt is not always hurt. They perpetuate a havoc driven hatred and emptiness. The *Complaint of the Improper* is not a true authentic cry, so make sure you are not one of them. Wolf criers are sometimes the wolves themselves.

> **When I hear men and women of God fumble through the Bible, committing biblical perjury as they manipulate the minds of people for their own personal gain, I am abhorred.**

THE CAUSE FOR INTERCESSION

Crying about something is one thing, but praying about a thing is something completely different. Many vices and variables influence situations that are designed for purpose and process. Oftentimes, many people tend to follow the consensus of the majority while overlooking the voice of the minority. As long as we are in this world, we will always have conflicts, confusion, and catastrophic circumstances that play into the experiences of the human life landscape. Life circumstances are more about *when* than it is about *if*. Time has a way of introducing us to experiences and encounters that are never listed on our day planner or agenda. Many problems and challenges face the ecumenical community, which, at times, are very embarrassing. We have scandals of every kind—man-made empires that are personality driven instead of God made churches that point people to the Redeeming Savior, Jesus the Christ. So the question becomes what are we going to do? We can't continue down the path of character assassinations and public media bashing, including barbershop and beauty shop trash talking. At some point, we're going to have to work toward a better good within ourselves.

> **Pastors will need to guard their hearts and actions more sacredly for the sake of the Kingdom of God agenda.**

The cause of intercession is the call of interception. We've got to start blocking these demonic kicks and tricks and start intercepting some of these conflicts before they touch down into the minds of people and create negative responses. Pastors will need to guard their hearts and actions more sacredly for the sake of the Kingdom of God agenda.

We need a listening environment that gives credibility to the crying of the people who wait in optimistic anticipation that consideration to their pain is going to be granted. We who are called to lead God's people must become the initiators of peace and prosperity for all of God's people. People have been wounded in ways we can't even imagine, and their trust in the Church, in many ways, has been compromised. But there yet remains a remnant that has never given up on the power of prayer. It is out of those prayers that this book was written. The prayers of the righteous always cause productive things to happen, even supernatural things. I believe that the Body of Christ is facing crucial times, but I also believe that these times are strategic moments designed by the creator to bring His Church from out of the shadows of egocentric leadership hijacking by people whose motives in ministry are self-centered.

I hope and pray these words have enlightened your aptitude and heightened your awareness in a positive and enriching way.

CHAPTER EIGHT

WOLVES IN SHEPHERDS' CLOTHING

In approaching carefully this chapter with another challenging thought of discussion, I realize I am treading in some deep waters that may be offensive to those who feel that we pastors should not be confronted in this manner. I agree that some criticisms hailed at pastors by some pundits have crossed the line of abuse and misuse of their platforms when they speak harshly of preachers. Such is not the case with me because I will never step outside of the integrity of my position by lending my voice to criticisms that are not shared in love. Being loud and brash is not how we should make correction of those things that do not represent the integrity of the preacher. However, I also will not compromise the truth just so I can be politically correct or appreciated and affirmed by people whom I share ecclesiastical collegiality. Truth is the only path to freedom in any scenario, and as a man of God, is that truth will always be my course and cause for confrontation. Truth will always trump evil and the evil intentions that plague the religious community. In order to get to that truth, we must follow the person of truth, Jesus our Christ who is our example.

We have unfortunately witnessed too many public scandals that affect all of us who are called of God, and these issues must be addressed. Nothing that we've seen is alien to the Scriptures. And the truth of the matter is we have not seen all that we are going to see. My assignment is to do all that I can to help in the purging of the pulpit and within the congregation of God's assembly so our voices and the visual perceptions of the Church can be restored. The world needs our help. That's why Jesus called us to go into the world, so we can impact it in a positive way. If shepherds who are called of God do not come to a place of correction, our impact in the world is going to be completely diluted and of no effect. There are predators in some of our pulpits, and we must address this spirit of deception unless we all be judged unfairly due to the ungodly antics of those who are acting recklessly with their roles as pastors and prophets. As a pastor, I have been warned on many occasions to beware of wolves in sheep's clothing, but I never thought I'd have to one day address the issue of wolves in shepherds' clothing. The reality is undeniable, and I would have to misrepresent the call of God and the anointing on my life if I were to overlook this evolving issue in the Body of Christ.

There are predators in some of our pulpits, and we must address this spirit of deception unless we all be judged unfairly due to the ungodly antics of those who are acting recklessly with their roles as pastors and prophets.

The Word of God is punctuated with many narratives where God, through his prophets and apostles, had to address these predatory tactics and tendencies of negligent shepherds/pastors. You will see the correlation and synopsis between the Old and New Testament literature that relates to predatory leadership in the religious and Christian community and culture. Much of these predatory issues were over the greed of money and personal gain. Observe how the Apostle Paul encouraged and instructed his young pastor son Timothy in these matters:

> "If the masters are believers, that is no excuse for being disrespectful. Those slaves should work all the harder because their efforts are helping other believers who are well loved. Teach these things, Timothy, and encourage everyone to obey them. Some people may contradict our teaching, but these are the wholesome teachings of the Lord Jesus Christ. These teachings promote a godly life. Anyone who teaches something different is arrogant and lacks understanding. Such a person has an unhealthy desire to quibble over the meaning of words. This stirs up arguments ending in jealousy, division,

slander, and evil suspicions. These people always cause trouble. Their minds are corrupt, and they have turned their backs on the truth. To them, a show of godliness is just a way to become wealthy. Yet true godliness with contentment is itself great wealth. After all, we brought nothing with us when we came into the world, and we can't take anything with us when we leave it. So if we have enough food and clothing, let us be content. But people who long to be rich fall into temptation and are trapped by many foolish and harmful desires that plunge them into ruin and destruction. For the love of money is the root of all kinds of evil. And some people, craving money, have wandered from the true faith and pierced themselves with many sorrows." — 1 Timothy 6:2–10 NLT

Jesus taught this principle to his disciples in Mark 4:19 when he was teaching them kingdom principles to understand and to live by.

And the cares of this world and the deceitfulness of riches, and the lusts of other things entering in, choke the word, and it becometh unfruitful. — Mark 4:19, KJV

Here are a few more Scriptures to be considered:

Your leaders are like wolves who tear apart their victims. They actually destroy people's lives for money!" And your prophets cover up for them by announcing false visions and making lying predictions. They say, 'My message is from the Sovereign LORD,' when the LORD hasn't spoken a single word to them." — Ezekiel 22:27–28, NLT

And the word of the Lord came unto me, saying, Son of man, prophesy against the shepherds of Israel, prophesy, and say unto them, Thus saith the Lord God unto the shepherds; Woe be to the shepherds of Israel that do feed themselves! Should not the shepherds feed the flocks? Ye eat the fat, and ye clothe you with the wool, ye kill them that are fed: but ye feed not the flock. The diseased have ye not strengthened, neither have ye healed that which was sick, neither have ye bound up that which was broken, neither have ye brought again that which was driven away, neither have ye sought that which was lost; but with force and with cruelty have ye ruled them. And they were scattered, because there is no shepherd: and they became meat to all the beasts of the field, when they were scattered. My sheep wandered through all the mountains, and upon every high hill: yea, my flock was scattered upon all the face of the earth, and none did search or seek after them. Therefore, ye shepherds, hear the word of the Lord; As I live, saith the Lord God, surely because my flock became a prey, and my flock became meat to every beast of the field, because there was no shepherd, neither did my shepherds search for my flock, but the shepherds fed themselves, and fed not my flock; Therefore, O ye shepherds, hear the word of the Lord; Thus saith the Lord God; Behold, I am against the shepherds; and I will require my flock at their hand, and cause them to cease from feeding the flock; neither shall the shepherds feed themselves any more; for I will deliver my flock from their mouth, that they may not be meat for them. — Ezekiel 34:1–10, KJV

"Jerusalem is doomed, that corrupt, rebellious city that oppresses its own people. It has not listened to the LORD or accepted his discipline. It has not put its trust in the LORD or asked for his help. Its officials are like roaring lions; its judges are like hungry wolves, too greedy to leave a bone until morning. The prophets are irresponsible and treacherous; the priests defile what is sacred, and twist the law of God to their own advantage. But the LORD is still in the city; he does what is right and never what is wrong. Every morning without fail, he brings justice to his people. And yet the unrighteous people there keep on doing wrong and are not ashamed." — Zephaniah 3:1–5, GNB

Pay careful attention to yourselves and to all the flock, in which the Holy Spirit has made you overseers, to care for the church of God, which he obtained with his own

> blood. I know that after my departure fierce wolves will come in among you, not sparing the flock; and from among your own selves will arise men speaking twisted things, to draw away the disciples after them. Therefore be alert, remembering that for three years I did not cease night or day to admonish every one with tears. And now I commend you to God and to the word of his grace, which is able to build you up and to give you the inheritance among all those who are sanctified. I coveted no one's silver or gold or apparel. You yourselves know that these hands ministered to my necessities and to those who were with me. In all things I have shown you that by working hard in this way we must help the weak and remember the words of the Lord Jesus, how he himself said, 'It is more blessed to give than to receive.'" — Acts 20:27–35, ESV

As you can see, the Bible is very clear and proves there's nothing new under the sun or to the Son. For the most part, the problem is the absence due to silence and compromise of the true apostolic and prophetic voice of discipline, confrontation and correction within the Body of Christ. The uprise of social media and the awareness and attentiveness of a new generation of people have brought many of these issues into the forefront of public scrutiny. My assignment is not to uncover what has already been uncovered. I am also not called to cover up these issues through some kind of loyalty to silence. I want to see the integrity of the clergy restored on every level, even though I know we are all flesh of clay, but we have an assignment that mandates uncompromised discipline. Let's look transparently and truthfully at the difference between Wolves as Shepherds and True Shepherds.

A. Wolves as Shepherds:

1. They Disguise Themselves:

To disguise yourself is to camouflage your natural appearance, so people won't recognize the real you. It is also the obscured presentation of your true state of character. It's oxymoronic to me to be formulating these definitions as an attributing commentary to the literary conversation and discussion of the shepherd, who is called of God to lead his people. However, some people have lost their way along the way and have foolishly fraternized themselves to beliefs that are absolutely contrary to the

Word and Will of God. A thirsty flesh that is not disciplined, along with personal aspirations and lusts that do not merge synergistically and theologically with God's call and commands, will produce fallen shepherds. These masked ministers who hide behind pretentious motives will go to great lengths to conceal their true character. Many of them are not even chosen of God; some of them are self-appointed, and others are elected by the religious systems that choose their leaders by resumes and credit scores, instead of righteousness of character. Even then, good people do turn to bad enticements in many ways, but they themselves are not totally bad; they, unfortunately, made some wrong turns in their lives that have caused them not to get back on the right road. If you feed your greed, you will build an enemy within you that is on a mission to destroy the purity of your soul. Temptation always appeals to your weaknesses, not your strengths, and if you do not initiate godly judgment when those temptations appear, you will find yourself in a ball of confusion. The Apostle James wrote these words of constructive clarity in James chapter one verses thirteen through fourteen:

> **A thirsty flesh that is not disciplined, along with personal aspirations and lusts that do not merge synergistically and theologically with God's call and commands, will produce fallen shepherds.**

"**Let no man say when he is tempted, I am tempted of God: for God cannot be tempted with evil, neither tempteth he any man: But every man is tempted, when he is drawn away of his own lust, and enticed**" James 1:13–14, KJV.

People who disguise themselves also deceive themselves because they believe they can cover up who they are when who they truly are will never stay under cover. But, unfortunately, some men and women of God perpetrate their persona at the expense of manipulating people to follow their demonic influenced scams. We have seen these scams far too many times in the Church, and we believers should be tired of it; I know that many people in the world are. As an apostolic leader, I am lending my voice through this writing to discourage and defeat this destructive form of leadership from within the Body of Christ. This is why the ministry of the Holy Spirit and the gifts that he imparts to believers is a mandate of necessity. The Holy Spirit in the believer and the ministry work of the Holy Spirit within the Church serve as a spiritual antibody and agent that immunizes people and place. This makes them spiritually healthy with the ability to discern false people and false plots that come to destroy the work of that local assembly. Disguised people always seek out desperate people who have a zeal for God, but no true knowledge of God. This makes such people easily deceived and taken advantage of.

2. They Deceive the Sheep:

To deceive people is to give a false impression by presenting something as truth or valid that is actually false and invalid. I will regretfully say this again: *deceive* is not a word that should be the common character definition of people who profess to be Christlike. These deceivers can become an anomalous of unequivocal persuasion and perception that misrepresents them in the house of God. These people do what they do against the goodwill of true godliness. They are opposers of the truth of God, and at some point, they will be judged by God. It is impossible to continue to get away with deceiving God's people through the manipulation of deceit. In the twenty-fourth chapter of Matthew, Jesus is sharing with his disciples some eschatological insight into the things that would happen as the End of the Age is approaching. Here is what he admonishes in verse five: **"See that no one leads you astray. For many will come in my name, saying, 'I am the Christ,' and they will lead many astray."** In verse eleven, he reiterates that same message: **"And many false prophets will arise and lead many astray."**

Many of these deceiving wolves will falsely present themselves as being full of God and righteousness and will attempt to over rate their anointing and biblical and spiritual aptitude with a lot of hyperbole preaching. They lack homiletic integrity and will appeal to the emotions of people through what is perceived to be prophetic by those who don't have the knowledge of the prophetic. Some of them are only purse-snatching wallet-grabbing scammers who insult true biblical-based prosperity. Anyone who preaches prosperity and wealth by faith alone and without labor is not holding true to the Gospel message. Wealth without work and sacrifice of sweat is false advertisement and carries no weight to it. Jesus didn't give us faith to get wealth; he gave us faith to become focused on following him into the truth, which is to bring us into the knowledge of him and his Father. Wealth is not meant to be our pursuit; the Kingdom of God is to be our pursuit. Here is what God told Joshua in regards to his success and prosperity:

> Only be thou strong and very courageous, that thou mayest observe to do according to all the law, which Moses my servant commanded thee: turn not from it to the right hand or to the left, that thou mayest pros-

> per whithersoever thou goest. This book of the law shall not depart out of thy mouth; but thou shalt meditate therein day and night, that thou mayest observe to do according to all that is written therein: for then thou shalt make thy way prosperous, and then thou shalt have good success. — Joshua 1:7–8, KJV

As you can see, a divine principle and standard says that if we obey God, follow His Word, and never compromise the instructions, then prosperity and success will be the reward from that obedience. Don't chase the gifts; chase the giver. Don't chase the blessing; pursue the blesser. As a result, you'll have the blessing that makes one not just financially rich, but also spiritually, emotionally, and mentally rich—without adding sorrow to it. Faith doesn't pursue money; it pursues the Master himself, and He'll release everything that we need to live like He wants us to live.

It is true, however, that faith is the main component of the Christian hope and belief, but that faith must be clarified in its depth, not simplified by using it as tool to deceive people into following a scam-driven intent without question or proof. God even said for us to try him, test him, and prove him. None of us are God, so we must be tested for truth. I have a quote that says, "Anything that hasn't been tested is not ready to be tasted and is not worthy of being trusted." Many Scriptures warn us of this kind of predatory manipulation, too many to list here, but I will share a few that are in context and commonality with this discussion. You should also note that many of the deceivers that the Bible references are the people themselves, not just the pastors and prophets. I do not reference that group here because they are not the topic of this discussion.

> No one who puts their trusts in you will ever be disgraced, but disgrace comes to those who try to deceive others. — Psalm 25:3, NLT

> Beware of false prophets, which come to you in sheep's clothing, but inwardly they are ravening wolves. Ye shall know them by their fruits. — Matthew 7:15

> For false messiahs and prophets will rise up and perform signs and wonders so as to deceive, if possible, even God's chosen ones. — Matthew 24:24, NLT

> What sorrow awaits them! For they follow in the footsteps of Cain, who killed his brother. Like Balaam, they deceive people for money. And like Korah, they perish in their rebellion. — Jude 1:11, NLT

> I will not allow deceivers to serve in my house, and liars will not stay in my house. — Psalm 101:7, NLT

3. They Divide the Flock to Favor Themselves:

To divide something is to separate it into two or more pieces or fractions. In this discourse, I shed some light of truth on how predatory people create intentional friction to cause a fraction that separates the weak from the strong. Unfortunately, the weak sheep find themselves as prey to the predator while the strong, who are able to see through the scam and scheme, are seen to be the evil opposition. Pastors who become intimidated by strong people, but empowered by weak people, are insecure at their core, so they manipulate to avoid being exposed. They make the weak feel wanted and needed, but that need is being met at a great price and advantage that serves only the good and advancement of the predatory-type leader. Anytime someone appeals to your weakness, without the intent to help you to become stronger, that person is using you and is not interested in your total growth.

> **Pastors who become intimidated by strong people, but empowered by weak people, are insecure at their core, so they manipulate to avoid being exposed.**

This, however, is not to be seen as a form of stereotypical pastoral leadership within the Church majority; it's only meant to address those persons to whom this applies. I am competent enough and have been in ministry long enough to know that this is not the common denominator or standard and strategy of the typical pastoring shepherd. I wrote this book to expose this evil and to educate those who continue to become victimized by that small majority. One small match can start a fire that will burn down a forest and destroy communities of property. So while these predators may be a small fraction of leaders, there still remains a fire of destruction that has set a negative image that all good pastors have to contend with in the world's culture of perception and criticism. Some may say in cynical defense that who cares about what the world thinks. But we all should care because the world is where the seed of the Word of God is to be planted and cultivated, so the Kingdom of God can have a dominant influence into what goes on within it.

Being an animal advocate and lover, I watch *Animal Kingdom* on television whenever I get the chance, and I've learned some things about predatory animals that are metaphors of the way some leaders handle the sheep of God's flock. One of the observations I've made is that most of these jungle predators hunt for food with careful strategy. They usually go after the youngest and weakest in the herd; they do this by trying to catch the young animal that drifts away from its parents. The parents represent strength and stability with the ability to withstand certain attacks on the flock or herd. The Bible shares this principle in 1 Peter 5:8, where the Apostle Peter writes, **"Be sober, be vigilant; because your adversary the devil, as a roaring lion, walketh about, seeking whom he may devour."** Notice that the biblical text talks of the roaring lion, the roaming lion, and the researching lion. I break down these attributes for your observation and consideration.

    A. **The Roaring Lion:** The lion's roar is designed to create a panic within its prey; it will roar as a method of intimidation. It understands that if it can get the prey it is after to become fearful, the prey becomes weakend in heart and strength. Fear takes the fight out of the one who is afraid and increases the fight in the one doing the roaring. Unfortunately, some preachers and leaders use this intimidating style of leadership for the purpose of gaining control to themselves. They use the preaching moment to beat the sheep down while raising their own level of authoritative dominance, frightening people into submission to their service. I realize this sounds difficult to believe, but it is true, and it exists within the Church assembly, even though it is neither a Jesus type of leadership nor is it a Holy Spirit type of leading. Pastors are called to lead their people by inspiration from the Holy Spirit, not by intimidation, which is a carnal and bullying style that comes from some form of abuse-driven insecurity. Inspiring people will lead them to become the best they can be; intimidating people empowers only the bitterness and brutality of the one doing the intimidating. You can't nurture sheep through Bible bullying; you only stagnate, frustrate and divide them because some sheep are not going to be intimidated.

B. **The Roaming Lion:** The roaming lion does not settle into one place. It is often on the move, on the hunt, and looking for the right place to make its attack. Like the lion, the wolf in shepherds' clothing is a roamer, sometimes traveling miles and days. These animals are very calculating and will, for instance, use the climate in its calculation. A wolf knows that animals with hoofs have a hard time moving through snow, so it tracks down its prey into the snow just to have an advantage in the killing process. Not to make this a referendum on animal life, it is incumbent upon us to understand biblical metaphors. It is on this understanding that discernment is developed in order to avoid deception from the enemies of this world. Some men and women roam from place to place, city to city, church to church, trying to find a comfortable place to harbor and hide as they plot their next church heist. I've seen it. I've experienced it, and I've had to confront and remove it from around me. This happens at all levels of Church leadership—in senior leadership as well as subordinate leadership. Some associate pastors prey on the sheep within the church where they serve under a senior pastor. The spirit of the roaming lion is akin to satan himself, and we see him acknowledging it to God in Job 1:6–7: **"Now there was a day when the sons of God came to present themselves before the Lord, and Satan came also among them. And the Lord said unto Satan, Whence comest thou? Then Satan answered the Lord, and said, From going to and fro in the earth, and from walking up and down in it"** KJV. A strategy is behind these roaming lions, wolves, and demonic influences, which I describe in the next attribute.

C. **The Researching Lion:** To research something is to study that thing in detail in order to gain knowledge of how it functions and learning its strengths and weaknesses. This is the strategy of the predatory type. The lion, as stated in 1 Peter 5:8, is said to be seeking whom it may devour. The lion roars and roams, but it studies its prey, watching for the most vulnerable, weakest, youngest, and oldest. The wolf in shepherds' clothing does the same thing, studying its prey. We learn the same thing in the Job narratives regarding satan, in which he stated he was going to and fro throughout the earth. God asked him if he had considered Job, the upright man, but satan said, **"He has a hedge around him."** Job was strong in every way. And in order for satan to attack him, he had to have him weakened to do so. That is the way of the predator, even in the pulpit. These people prey on the weakness of people, dividing the strong against the weak, just to give themselves a stronger position of influence. The wisdom of the predatory type instructs them to be strategic to ensure that what they go after they get. That's why they carefully select to their advantage. It's not to the advantage of their predatory intentions to try and manipulate people in their church who are wise, strong, spirit-filled, knowledgeable of the Word of God, and with the wisdom of discernment. They must go after the naive, unlearned, gullible, desperate, and insecure people who lack true spiritual depth and maturation. So in order to further the cause of scamming people, they have to divide the strong against the weak, and get the weak to form an allegiance with them. Oftentimes, what happens is that unethical pastors will ultimately split their church and start a new ministry. This is a pattern I've witnessed far too many times, and I'm sure some of you reading this book have witnessed the same. Be careful of leaders who try to divide you against other people within the ministry. Wherever the spirit of division exists and operates, you can be assured it is not being led by the spirit of good intention. God is the author of the united visions that are designed to prosper the people. He is not the author of divisive agendas that benefit only the leader who is concerned only with his or her own prosperity.

4. They Devour the Flock to Enrich Themselves:

To devour something is to prey upon it to the point of destroying it or drawing it until it has nothing else to give. This is the action of the guilty greedy who want it all to themselves for their own selfish and pleasurable consumptions. This behavior is the work of the flesh, not the work of the Spirit of God. The Apostle Paul addresses these spiritual malfeasances in the book of Galatians:

> For, brethren, ye have been called unto liberty; only use not liberty for an occasion to the flesh, but by love serve one another. For all the law is fulfilled in one word, even in this; Thou shalt love thy neighbour as thyself. But if ye bite and devour one another, take heed that ye be not consumed one of another. This I say then, Walk in the Spirit, and ye shall not fulfil the lust of the flesh. For

the flesh lusteth against the Spirit, and the Spirit against
the flesh: and these are contrary the one to the other:
so that ye cannot do the things that ye would. But if ye
be led of the Spirit, ye are not under the law. Now the
works of the flesh are manifest, which are these; Adul-
tery, fornication, uncleanness, lasciviousness, Idolatry,
witchcraft, hatred, variance, emulations, wrath, strife,
seditions, heresies, Envyings, murders, drunkenness,
revellings, and such like: of the which I tell you before,
as I have also told you in time past, that they which do
such things shall not inherit the kingdom of God. —
Galatians 5:13–21, KJV

Plato, in the first book of his Commonwealth, describes the office of a magistrate by saying, *"He should look upon himself as sustaining the office of a shepherd, that makes it his chief business to take care of his flock; not as if he were going to a feast to fill himself and satiate his appetite, or to a market to make what gain he can to himself."*

When there exist amongst the sheep devouring shepherds who are driven by their greed, the spiritual fortitude of the sheep is forever compromised. This is not what God intended when He appoints shepherds over his flocks. As I've stated in earlier chapters, don't feed off the sheep, lead the sheep and allow God to provide for you all the necessities for your life. We are seeing too much of this type of behavior in the Body of Christ and, at some point and in the Spirit and authority of Christ, we have to confront this spirit because that's exactly what it is. The Apostle Paul writes expressively to his young pastor son Timothy this prophetic forecast:

But the Spirit saith expressly, that in later times some
shall fall away from the faith, giving heed to seducing
spirits and doctrines of demons, through the hypocrisy
of men that speak lies, branded in their own conscience
as with a hot iron. — 1 Timothy 4:1–2

We are living in these times, and they just didn't start in recent years. The advancement of social media and the media in general have brought many of these kinds of misbehaviors to public view. These current times are exposing many of these predatory junkets who enjoy the pleasures of their flesh at the expense of someone else's hard work, money and sacrifice. For this form of plagiarizing to exist within the Church community is an insult to the doctrines of our Christ. The Bible has forewarned us of these kinds of people coming into the family of God for the purpose of their selfish gains. I close this segment by sharing scriptural references that support this position.

B. True Shepherds:

The following biblical narrative is a pastoral mandate that Jesus gives to Peter and a model to be mimicked by all pastors as it relates to how pastoral care should be provided for the sheep within the assembly of God's Kingdom Church. I also provide a descriptive outline that gives pointed particulars of my personal perspective regarding the role of the shepherd. Please note in verse fifteen that Jesus always feeds those who follow him—physical and spiritual food. He engaged himself into their physical and spiritual need, and this is the pattern of good pastorship responsibility:

> So when they had dined, Jesus saith to Simon Peter, Simon, son of Jonas, lovest thou me more than these? He saith unto him, Yea, Lord; thou knowest that I love thee. He saith unto him, Feed my lambs. He saith to him again the second time, Simon, son of Jonas, lovest thou me? He saith unto him, Yea, Lord; thou knowest that I love thee. He saith unto him, Feed my sheep. He saith unto him the third time, Simon, son of Jonas, lovest thou me? Peter was grieved because he said unto him the third time, Lovest thou me? And he said unto him, Lord, thou knowest all things; thou knowest that I love thee. Jesus saith unto him, Feed my sheep. — John 21:15–17

1. True Shepherds Care for the Sheep Tenderly:

As stated in earlier chapters, the care of the sheep is one that requires a depth of compassion that exceeds personality distinctions. Let me explain. Some pastors are not affectionately sensitive as others because of their personality type, which is not to suggest they don't care in their heart. However, I advocate that we don't pastor God's people based on personality, but responsibility and accountability to God. We must treat the sheep as Christ has instructed us. Love is an affection of unconditional attributes that propels a person to do for others what may not be within the norm of their comfort. Pastoring people will challenge the core of your values because you are held accountable for people who have so many different personality types and needs. When Jesus is questioning Peter's love for him, he is testing him and teaching him at the same time. When Peter, on the first line of questioning, answers yeah, Lord, you know that I love you, Jesus responded by saying feed my lambs. It is here that Jesus is teaching him pastoral principles. What he is saying, in essence, to Peter is tend to my sheep, pasture my young immature disciples. As an exegetical side note, he's affirming also Peter's ministry because of past difficulties and personal challenges that Peter faced after denying him. Of his own guilt, Peter felt disconnected, but Jesus was ministering to that spirit of self-condemnation.

The lesson Jesus is teaching Peter through the first line of questioning and instruction is for Peter as a pastor to understand the tenderness of the sheep. Now tenderness doesn't always mean lack of toughness, but it speaks to a cause or case of vulnerability within the sheep nature. With that in mind, Pastor Peter and any others who call themselves pastors, must handle the sheep with a tender intelligence and understanding. Discipline doesn't have to be rough; it can be done gently and tenderly. The objective is to cause the sheep to mature in a well-balanced way. When Jesus says "Feed," it is grammatically spoken as a present active imperative verb that implies a continual action. In other words, "Keep feeding them."

> **Pastoring people will challenge the core of your values because you are held accountable for people who have so many different personality types and needs.**

A couple of teaching lessons to notice and learn in these lines of questioning are that Jesus uses Peter's old name Simon when questioning him. This speaks to his fallen nature, not his transformation nature, which is under character reconstruction. Jesus does this three times to remind him of the three times he denied Jesus. This is not done as a form of intimidation, but to show Simon that even though he messed up, he's not beyond repair and restoration. Simon is going to have to love, nurture, and feed his sheep from the place of his new nature, not his old one. As pastors, you do not lead and feed God's people from the foundations of your human nature, but from the place of your spiritually renewed nature. Loving people like God loves them can never happen from our human nature but rather our spiritual nature. Sheep will bite you, and some will betray you, but you must never resort to your human nature. You must be mindful of how he restored you. I'll expound on this point as we progress toward the end of this chapter.

2. TRUE SHEPHERDS CARRY THE SHEEP WHEN THEY'RE TOO WOUNDED TO CARRY THEMSELVES:

> What man of you, having an hundred sheep, if he lose one of them, doth not leave the ninety and nine in the wilderness, and go after that which is lost, until he find it? And when he hath found it, he layeth it on his shoulders, rejoicing. And when he cometh home, he calleth together his friends and neighbours, saying unto them, Rejoice with me; for I have found my sheep which was lost. I say unto you, that likewise joy shall be in heaven over one sinner that repenteth, more than over ninety and nine just persons, which need no repentance. — Luke 15:4–7

A part of caring for the sheep involves carrying them in their times of stagnation when they struggle, are stranded from straying, and show stubbornness from not being submissive to leadership. Wounded sheep warrant a necessity within the Church to move to positive action. Oftentimes, as seen in the populated Church in which there is a lack of accountability and personal pastoral attentiveness, sheep get lost and go lagging. When this happens in the Church of today and pastors are attendance driven instead of attention driven, they oftentimes tend to neglect the sheep. The desire to be a big church in numbers takes priority over being a better church in nature. God expects us not to focus just on those who have it right and are meeting the mandates of the ministry organization. We need to have a mission within the Church that gives attention to the stragglers and the straying. Notice in the previous biblical narrative that Jesus is speaking and using a hypothetical punctuation perspective or questioning. Here, he is also making an imperative assumption, conclusion, and command—and not just a suggestion—that if a man discovers that one out of the hundred of his sheep goes missing, that shepherd

A part of caring for the sheep involves carrying them in their times of stagnation when they struggle, are stranded from straying, and show stubbornness from not being submissive to leadership.

should go looking for his one lost sheep. He also asserts the assumption that he search until he finds it, and once he finds it, he puts it on his shoulders and carries it to its place of restoration with the other sheep.

This is what true shepherds do. They are invested in the life of the sheep and will do whatever is necessary to ensure they get to where he intends for them to be. As pastors, you must provide within your church the tools and ministry-related vehicles of service that keep your people focused. Your vision to build and expand must not be prioritized by the property you own and buildings you build, but by the people you develop and mature into the Kingdom of God. The Kingdom of God agenda is not in anything of a material nature, but it is seen in the power and demonstration of the Spirit of God to totally transform the nature of people into the likeness of Christ. The main expenditure of the church budget must be spent on developing people, not building physical buildings for recreation, but building spiritual programs for re-creation.

When you are a shepherd who cares, you become also a shepherd who carries; this you can't do alone, but you must train and empower people to help you in this endeavor. Your security team and sports teams should never be bigger and more visible than your prayer team, your Christian education team, your outreach team, your evangelism team, and your discipleship team. I assert this observation, which may offend some, but I'd rather offend than pretend. The ways and means of the traditional and religious Church tend to bend toward their own vision than the vision of our Savior and Lord, Jesus Christ. We must carry the sheep not just when we bury the sheep, but we must carry them as a result of building them up to walk on their own. We have been given the ministry of Christ as a lifetime call, and we must never circumvent that call to appease the religious thirsty.

3. True Shepherds Cultivate the Sheep Through Personal Development Strategies:

Cultivation is the process of nurturing and development that is provided to the sheep for the purpose of fostering growth and maturity. As a shepherd, personal development of the sheep is what bonds them to the shepherd, and this creates a level of loyal support of and for the shepherd. Refining people is the art of making people better than they are currently. This process sometimes can mandate steady and stern discipline in order to bring out the best in people. Sheep who understand that the shepherd has their best interest at heart will usually submit by the Holy Spirit to the leadership that is over them. No greater joy have I experienced in my 37 years of pastoring than seeing the people whom I lead and have led grow in their walk with God.

4. True Shepherds Cover the Sheep Through the Same Process of Grace that God Has Afforded Them:

To cover the Lord's sheep is to afford them protection and security from the attack of predatory enemies who come in to steal, kill, and destroy them. Another form of this word *cover* is one that I favor, and it means to hold within range. We shepherds must have a passion of protection that provides healthy watch and care to ensure that the sheep remain in range of view, so obstacles and attacks may be avoided. But if not avoided, it gives the shepherd quick response to action, so the sheep can avoid being fatally harmed. Now this is impossible for a shepherd to do only in the physical or natural realm because this battle takes place in the spirit realm. It is through the ministry of prayer and spiritual warfare that the shepherd engages in battle. The Bible is clear that we do not war against things in the flesh or in the natural, but in the spiritual realms. This is why when we are challenged to deal with resisting sheep and sometimes lawless sheep who struggle in their flesh, we must not minister to them as condemning judges, but as merciful servants. The ministry of grace is afforded to all within the family of God, not just the shepherd. This is the manner by which the shepherd must manage his sheep. Grace should always abound and overrule all areas of sin, struggle and shame. I have learned the principle of the Prodigal Father, who loves his children unconditionally, even when they rebel and runaway from the principles of his teaching. The Prodigal Father is one who is always ready to receive, restore, and reward their prodigal children once they return from their personal wilderness. You can see this principle in the parable of the prodigal son that Jesus tells in Luke 15:11–24. It is a story of love and one of my favorite parables, and one that I live by. It is designed mainly to give us an understanding of the love and grace by which our heavenly Father receives and restores those who trust him.

To conclude this chapter, I further acknowledge there is never a true in-depth explanation as to why some men and women of God result to such ungodly measures when given the opportunity to lead an assembly of God's people. Those of us who are made aware of these predatory situations must speak out for the sake of the Kingdom of God and the integrity of the ministry that we all share together with Him. We are all a part of one big family of God, and when there are things of a corrupt nature that infiltrates that family, the mature must not be silent. Wolves in shepherds' clothing must be confronted by shepherds and spiritual leaders who walk in a true shepherd's grace and anointing.

CHAPTER NINE

IS THAT WHAT THAT SCRIPTURE MEANT? THE INTEGRITY OF PREACHING

Using correct biblical hermeneutics when referencing the Scriptures is what sustains the integrity of preaching and empowers, educates, and edifies those who are partakers of its truths. Preaching is not the platform for anyone to perform his or her misinterpretations of oratorical solecisms. It is, however, the place where God must be presented in His purest form, and His Word must not be compromised for the sake of some preacher's egotistical insecurity and need for attention. The message on prosperity and many of its teachings have been contextually compromised because of poor biblical exegesis. This chapter is a presentation of correction and uncompromised interpretation of Scriptures that relate to the subject of prosperity, riches, and wealth. I have discovered that many false teachers are twisting the Scriptures in order to enrich themselves while enslaving the sheep of God to false teachings. Just because you believe something to be true does not make it truth. You have to rightly divide the Word of God and not commit biblical perjury by making the Bible out to say and mean something that it neither says nor means.

Many pastors, unfortunately, have become prisoners to what they possess materially and not what they preach spiritually. The personal and preferred comforts of a preacher must never become the defense for overtaxing God's people. God did not call us to comfort; He called us to confrontation and sacrifice. The same sacrifices that we ask the people to make, we must be willing to make and, at times, even greater sacrifices. God will reward us, so let Him be the standard-bearer and icon in the people's eyes, and let us become servants in their eyes. It's time for us to remove our names and faces from the headlines of the media's scrutiny all because we don't have the discipline to live with a sobriety that allows us to be seen not as men and women of greed, but men and women of true spiritual power who also maintain humility. The Gospel that we preach is free, so why do we charge the people to hear it? A financial and business element is evident in ministry, but that financial and business element must not make us the sponge that absorbs it all for ourselves.

> **Many pastors, unfortunately, have become prisoners to what they possess materially and not what they preach spiritually.**

Public perception must be the considered ideological conception and reception of our intentions. We must ask ourselves, "What will my decisions echo to the people to whom I am called to lead?" No plane, house, car or any other material trinket is worth the dilution of our ecclesiastical integrity. We must, at all times, want people to see the Christ in us, not the cars in our driveways, the planes in our aircraft hangers, or the multiple houses in our real estate portfolios. Is it fair that we be expected to modify certain passions and pleasures for the sake of the gospel? Yes, it is fair. It is the life we have been called to. Besides, none of us will ever sacrifice what Jesus sacrificed, and the early Church apostles sacrificed for the sake of the Gospel. If Jesus is our true example, then why do we overlook the simplicity of his life and lifestyle? He himself said to those who would follow him, **"The foxes have holes and the birds of the air have nests, but the Son of man has nowhere to lay his head"** Matthew 8:20. The implication is simple, and it implies that comfort and convenience are not a guarantee if you decide to follow him. Read carefully and correctly what the Apostle Paul said to the Church at Philippi concerning their care of him:

> But I rejoiced in the Lord greatly, that now at the last your care of me hath flourished again; wherein ye were

> also careful, but ye lacked opportunity. Not that I speak in respect of want: for I have learned, in whatsoever state I am, therewith to be content. I know both how to be abased, and I know how to abound: everywhere and in all things I am instructed both to be full and to be hungry, both to abound and to suffer need. I can do all things through Christ which strengtheneth me. — Philippians 4:10–13

Paul is testifying to God's ability to sustain his servants, even when the people neglect to attend to them with noble and honorable care. We must never allow the people's care of us to define the integrity of our loyalty to preach and teach the Word without a selfish motive of intent. I know from personal experience that people will not always honor you in the way you may think they should. However, if you remain faithful to the call, then God will continue to care for you and elevate you in His timing. You don't have to manipulate to get what you anticipate. God will give you the strength to endure the rough times and will reward your sacrifice.

We must never allow the people's care of us to define the integrity of our loyalty to preach and teach the Word without a selfish motive of intent.

In this chapter, I want to examine Scriptures that are commonly used to promote the prosperity message, but those Scriptures are not referencing money. Let me make it clear that I do believe in prosperity, wealth and riches, but I believe it in its proper ethical context. And when it comes to the Bible being used as a reference, I definitely believe in the contextual integrity of Scriptures. The Bible is to be preached and taught, line upon line and precept upon precept, with proper interpretation, revelation and illumination. The reason why some people resort to biblical piracy is because they have an agenda that causes them to preach and teach what is false, so they can gain what is real and valuable. In other words, many false teachers are getting rich off false representations of the Scriptures. They bewitch the minds of desperate people who live off the words of preachers whom they trust and are impressed with. Many people never pause to ask, "How are these Scriptures making preachers rich, but leaving so many other people broke?" You see, it is easy to tell a mass group of people that it is better to give than to receive when you are the recipient of what they give. When Luke writes this Scripture in Acts

20, Paul was referencing giving to the weak and needy and to support the service of the ministry.

This financial over-taxation for the preacher's personal relaxation and comfort is a hustle of dishonor, and it needs to stop, especially when we watch the sheep die in desperation and expectation for a blessing to come through for them that never comes. This is not consistent with the biblical mannerisms of the shepherd. In the Bible, the shepherd is the one who makes the greatest sacrifice. Read John 10 and Psalm 23 and you will see the example of how shepherds should govern and care for the sheep. Unfortunately, we are living through times when the prosperity of the preacher is way ahead of his or her sheep. I'll never understand or accept the idea of the shepherd enjoying luxurious lifestyles on the back of the sheep while most of them live day to day, supporting these expensive lifestyle mandates that are pressed on them by supposed anointed men and women of God. That's not how anointed men and women of God conduct themselves. The anointing is for service, not for material substance and prominence. According to Luke 4:18, we're supposed to be setting people free from captivity and bondage, healing their broken hearts, and giving sight to the physically and spiritually blind.

Unfortunately, people are being scammed, and so much financial hardship and greed is blindly leading people down paths that have no purposeful destiny at their end. All we see, for the most part, are dead-end promises and delayed detours that keep people moving, but are taking them nowhere. There are secular business principles to wealth, riches and prosperity, as well as biblical principles that can be applied to your life in order to achieve wealth. But for men and women of God to suggest that faith and giving is the key to their financial prosperity is to ignore the biblical principle that says if you don't work, then you don't eat. And if you try eating and not working, you're going either to starve or to steal—now that's not a part of the Scripture, but part of my sarcasm.

> Wealth gotten by vanity shall be diminished; But he that gathereth by labor shall have increase. — Proverbs 13:11

> "And now, dear brothers and sisters, we give you this command in the name of our Lord Jesus Christ: Stay away from all believers who live idle lives and don't follow the tradition they received from us. For you know

that you ought to imitate us. We were not idle when we were with you. We never accepted food from anyone without paying for it. We worked hard day and night so we would not be a burden to any of you. We certainly had the right to ask you to feed us, but we wanted to give you an example to follow. Even while we were with you, we gave you this command: "Those unwilling to work will not get to eat." Yet we hear that some of you are living idle lives, refusing to work and meddling in other people's business. We command such people and urge them in the name of the Lord Jesus Christ to settle down and work to earn their own living. As for the rest of you, dear brothers and sisters, never get tired of doing good. Take note of those who refuse to obey what we say in this letter. Stay away from them so they will be ashamed. Don't think of them as enemies, but warn them as you would a brother or sister." — 2 Thessalonians 3:6–15, NLT

Faith giving is a principle used by many Word of faith teachers, but there is often a thin threading of theological and biblical interpretation that is used to validate its doctrinal position. The way this doctrine is interpreted, at times, is in some ways a misinterpretation of the Scriptures supported by psychological tactics that appeal to people's emotions and their eager desired will to escape quickly their financial disparities. Faith must never be the excuse for foolish judgments and decisions. If you have to pay your mortgage or rent and buy food for your family and some preacher tells you to sow that money into the kingdom and trust God to provide for you, that person is a liar and is not hearing from God. First of all, you need to know that the church organization is not the Kingdom of God; it is a carrier of the Kingdom of God message. First, the Kingdom of God is an idea of thinking that conforms to the righteous standards of God by doing things God's way. Second, God does not require foolish loyalty, only faithful and obedient loyalty from those who profess to love Him. Let me lay out for you an apological argument based on Scripture that gives clarity to my position. The Widow Woman in Zarephath in 1 Kings 17:8–16 had her faith in God challenged, but the Man of God, Prophet Elijah, did not require her to give him everything she had, only a portion of it. And if you study the text correctly and in its entirety, you will note that God told Elijah to go to Zarephath for He had commanded a widow woman to sustain him there. So when

Elijah gives the woman instructions, he's really conveying a message that, in some way, either defines or confirms something in this woman. He asks her for water, and she complies, even though water is in short supply because of famine due to no rain. It was only when he asks her for some of what she was cooking that she hesitated with reserved resistance. But when he says that she should feed him first and then her son and herself, with the promise of God's provision regarding her obedience, she complies. In the end, she never wanted for oil and meal again even while the famine lasted. This biblical narrative is not a present command of repetition and requirements. This principle is designed to teach us of God's provisions, not man's promises. Remember, Elijah says nothing of what he would provide, but of what God would provide. Even though God said He had commanded a woman to sustain him, Elijah is not the person who determined what she must do; God determined it. Preachers, don't play with the principles or perpetuate a particular Bible story to pad your pockets. If you want everything that Elijah received in this passage, then you must do everything Elijah did to be in this position with God. Every Bible story is neither yours to repeat nor yours to reap from, but to remember in tough times.

> **First of all, you need to know that the church organization is not the Kingdom of God; it is a carrier of the Kingdom of God message.**

The Scripture narrative of the Widow's Mite in Luke 21:1–4 has oftentimes been used to compel and convince people with little to live on to sacrifice what they have so God takes notice of them and blesses them. However, this Scripture is not, in any way, telling people to give their all in an offering to support the ministry of a church or its minister. As a matter of truth, Jesus did not ask this woman to give all she had. She was compelled within her own heart of persuasion to give it, and Jesus recognized it, but he did not require it. The point he was making was more about the principle of equal sacrifice, not equal giving. Jesus made the observation that many people gave out of their abundance, but she gave out of her lack and poverty. He goes on in that chapter to lay out prophetic and eschatological discourse. He even warns there will arise men declaring to be who they are not, and that disciples make certain they are not deceived and led astray. To me it sounds just like some of today's scammers and deceivers who are abusing God's people, all for fortune and fame.

Even if you don't believe my position of thinking, you have to understand that these stories do not represent in any way a standard of giving for all people in impoverished situations. You can learn life principles from other people's experiences, but those experiences don't have to become your life practice. If God doesn't move on your heart, or if your heart is not moved to give something above what you've already determined to give, then don't give it; no matter who asks for it, don't give it. No man has the power to cause increase. It is a biblical principle that one man plants, another man waters, but it is God, who is not a man, who gives the increase, period. It is God who supplies and provides, so allow only Him to determine what you should give or shouldn't give. God does not want his preachers, pastors and shepherds flying on elaborate planes and driving in elaborate cars while His sheep are asked to give offerings so we can afford these luxuries while they are walking. I don't believe it, and I don't practice it, and I have Jesus as my example.

To perpetuate and pervert the promises of God for our lives down to our material possessions is a misrepresentation of the Bible, the author who inspired it, and the scribes and writers who penned it.

Here is why I judge this doctrine in the way that I do with such biblical caution. Faith is a major component of a life with God, who mandates faith as the manner by which we must approach Him. Hebrews chapter eleven verse six says, **"But without faith, it is impossible to please him: for he that cometh to God must believe that he is and that he is a rewarder of them that diligently seek him."** So faith in God is essential, but some teachers and preachers of the Word of God believe that absolute faith alone can produce wealth and prosperity, but I don't believe that. I believe faith without works or correspondent action is useless. Salvation is free, but being a Christian is not; one must do work to comply with that belief. A lot of Scriptures in which faith is required as it relates to prosperity is more about spiritual wealth and spiritual riches than it is about material and financial riches. **God is more concerned about the quality of your character than He is about the quantity of your cash.** The wealth of the Kingdom of God is not about money; it's about righteousness and obedience. Faith is the manner by which we seek the person of God, not the purse or possessions of God. **"For the kingdom of God is not meat and drink; but righteousness, and peace, and joy in the Holy Ghost"**

Romans 14:17, KJV. Our life in Christ is spiritual, not material; our human nature needs and lives on natural and material resources of the earth. Sometimes, those needs cross the line of normalcy and necessity and fall in line with greed and uncontrollable lusts. Mark 4:19 affirms this: **"and the cares of the world, and the deceitfulness of riches and the lust of other things entering in, choke the word, and it becometh unfruitful."**

This is why a life in Christ mandates a transformation of the mind. **"And be not conformed to this world: but be ye transformed by the renewing of your mind, that ye may prove what is that good, and acceptable, and perfect, will of God"** Romans 12:2, KJV. The perfect will of God is the honest, determined, conclusive and actual will of God for the lives of those who pursue a life in Him. To perpetuate and pervert the promises of God for our lives down to our material possessions is a misrepresentation of the Bible, the author who inspired it, and the scribes and writers who penned it. All of God's children are rich in Him, but not all of God's children will be rich with material wealth. This is an error of the truth that has many people living and giving of their financial resources into ministries and ministers with the hope that God is going to enrich them financially for doing so. Let me be clear when I say that the joy of giving is the joy in giving, period. It is not some anticipated notion that every time I give, my return is always going to be cash. God rewards our giving in many ways beyond monetary. God loves cheerful givers, and He will always give seed to those who sow with a pure intent of heart and mind. Read the following Scripture in its entirety and understand that the offering discussed was not for the coffers of the pastor or for the building fund of the church, but for what has been called the Macedonia cry. This offering's purpose was to give support to the unfortunate, not the fortunate. Although we can employ a good principle on giving when opportunities arrive to support the needs of the poor, when these offerings are being taken to enrich the already rich, then it's an abomination to float Scriptures behind such things being misrepresented.

> But this I say, He that soweth sparingly shall reap also sparingly; and he that soweth bountifully shall reap also bountifully. Let each man do according as he hath purposed in his heart: not grudgingly, or of necessity: for God loveth a cheerful giver. And God is able to make all grace abound unto you; that ye, having always all sufficiency in everything, may abound unto every good

> work: as it is written, He hath scattered abroad, he hath given to the poor; His righteousness abideth forever. And he that supplieth seed to the sower and bread for food, shall supply and multiply your seed for sowing, and increase the fruits of your righteousness: ye being enriched in everything unto all liberality, which worketh through us thanksgiving to God. For the ministration of this service not only filleth up the measure of the wants of the saints, but aboundeth also through many thanksgivings unto God; seeing that through the proving of you by this ministration they glorify God for the obedience of your confession unto the gospel of Christ, and for the liberality of your contribution unto them and unto all; while they themselves also, with supplication on your behalf, long after you by reason of the exceeding grace of God in you. Thanks be to God for his unspeakable gift. — 2 Corinthians 9:6–15, ASV

As a matter of biblical truth, God does not want his children worrying over how their needs are going to be met, especially when your job's salary is not always adequate for what you need to care for your family and yourself. He has a kingdom formula that works for those who live their lives by the standards of the Kingdom of God. He does have the power to persuade things into your favor, so your needs will be met. Jesus spoke the following words in this regard:

> Be not therefore anxious, saying, What shall we eat? or, What shall we drink? or, Wherewithal shall we be clothed? For after all these things do the Gentiles seek; for your heavenly Father knoweth that ye have need of all these things. But seek ye first his kingdom, and his righteousness; and all these things shall be added unto you. — Matthew 6:31–33, ASV

Don't ever forget that He who makes the promise is also He who makes the provisions. Know God for yourself, and know his Word for yourself. In this way, you guard yourself against the predatory practices of those who disregard biblical integrity.

> The thief cometh not, but for to steal, and to kill, and to destroy: I am come that they might have life, and that they might have it more abundantly. — John 10:10, KJV

Jesus is referencing the life that the Good Shepherd gives to the sheep, which is eternal life as well as a blossoming life. This Scripture is oftentimes presented in the context of wealth and riches when, in fact, money and riches never define the good life that God wants us to have. This life is a life of peace, joy and prosperity beyond material possessions. If such was the case, every believer would be rich, but all believers are not rich, so we must not preach a gospel that implies that because that's not God's eternal plan or promise for His people. There are poor people or just people in general who serve God and never make money a matter of their relationship with Him. It doesn't mean they don't have faith, or that they are are out of the will of God. When we perpetuate this prosperity message as the golden rule or the thing that validates God's goodness, we are teaching a false gospel.

As a matter of biblical truth, God does not want his children worrying over how their needs are going to be met.

When the Bible speaks of the poor, it does not always speak of them in a negative connotation, but it cautions us on how we handle them because judgment will come upon those who do. Those of us in the Body of Christ who are blessed to experience financial wealth are admonished to care for the poor. The problem in the world is not always the lazy poor, but the stingy and selfish rich who live under a cloud and code of greed. Study the following Scriptures for yourself:

> He gives prosperity to the poor and protects those who suffer. — Job 5:11, NLT

> Remember the Lord your God. He is the one who gives you power to be successful, in order to fulfill the covenant he confirmed to your ancestors with an oath. — Deuteronomy 8:18, NLT

> He told me, Cornelius, your prayer has been heard, and your gifts to the poor have been noted by God. — Acts 10:31, NLT

> He that hath pity upon the poor lendeth to the Lord;
> and that which he hath given will he pay him again. —
> Proverbs 19:17

The Bible does not promise wealth as many faith believers promote it to be. Being a Christian does not in any way guarantee that you will have a good job, wealth, freedom from debt, or avoid financial challenges. If people stop giving to many of these persons who teach such heresy, their lives and their self-made kingdoms would crumble. Do not misrepresent Jeremiah 29:11, which states, **"For I know the plans I have for you, 'declares the Lord,' plans to prosper you and not to harm you, plans to give you hope and a future"** NIV. The Hebrew word *prosper* in this context means completeness, peace, safety, health, satisfaction or blessings. Nothing in this Scripture talks solely about money. Now, it's a good talking point for people to use. But in proper context, it's talking about the outcome of the children of Israel concerning their captivity in Babylon due to their disobedience. God is telling them that even though they were responsible for their current state, He was still going to fulfill His promise to them. Read the whole chapter and study all of the content. Don't just grab a Scripture from a whole chapter to establish a doctrine.

As I stated before, some of God's people are rich, and some of His people are poor, but if the rich do right by their wealth, God will use them to help those who are experiencing poverty to live a much better life. Proverbs 22:2 says, **"Rich and poor have this in common: The Lord is the Maker of them all"** NIV. No, I am not suggesting that God made them poor, but they became poor. God doesn't favor one over another. While talking to his disciples in Luke 6:20–26, Jesus declared the following:

> Blessed are you who are poor, for your is the kingdom
> of God. Blessed are you who hunger now, for you will
> be satisfied. Blessed are you who weep now, for you will
> laugh. "Blessed are you when people hate you, when
> they exclude you and insult you and reject your name

> as evil, because of the Son of Man. "Rejoice in that day and leap for joy, because great is your reward in heaven. For that is how their ancestors treated the prophets. "But woe to you who are rich, for you have already received your comfort. Woe to you who are well fed now, for you will go hungry. Woe to you who laugh now, for you will mourn and weep. Woe to you when everyone speaks well of you, for that is how their ancestors treated the false prophets." — Luke 6:20–26, NIV

The Rich Young Ruler is yet another collaborative story that gives clarity to the true biblical significance and proper perspective of God's view on wealth and the poor. Here's a young man who, according to his own account of admission, was a keeper of the commandments of God and had plenty of wealth. But Jesus told him that he was still lacking something significant:

> And, behold, one came and said unto him, Good Master, what good thing shall I do, that I may have eternal life? And he said unto him, "Why callest thou me good? There is none good but one, that is, God: but if thou wilt enter into life, keep the commandments." He saith unto him, "Which?" Jesus said, "Thou shalt do no murder, Thou shalt not commit adultery, Thou shalt not steal, Thou shalt not bear false witness, "Honour thy father and thy mother:" and, "Thou shalt love thy neighbour as thyself." The young man saith unto him, "All these things have I kept from my youth up: what lack I yet?" Jesus said unto him, "If thou wilt be perfect, go and sell that thou hast, and give to the poor, and thou shalt have treasure in heaven: and come and follow me." But when the young man heard that saying, he went away sorrowful: for he had great possessions. Then said Jesus unto his disciples, "Verily I say unto you, that a rich man shall hardly enter into the kingdom of heaven. And again I say unto you, it is easier for a camel to go through the eye of a needle, than for a rich man to enter into the kingdom of God." When his disciples heard it, they were exceedingly amazed, saying, "Who then can be saved?" But Jesus beheld them, and said unto them,

> "With men this is impossible; but with God all things are possible." — Matthew 19:16–26

Please note that the disciples whom Jesus chose didn't follow him to get rich. They followed Jesus to become enriched. What an example for us to follow because there is so much for those who are called or say they are called to learn about being on the Lord's side. There is too much hype about the glamour of being a preacher or pastor. Ministry is not for our glamour, but for His glory.

> Beloved, I wish above all things that thou mayest prosper and be in health, even as thy soul prospereth. — 3 John 1:2, KJV

This is one of the most common and popular Scriptures used when referencing financial prosperity. However, this particular Scripture is a salutatory greeting from John to his beloved friend Gaius. He is not wishing him financial prosperity. He is actually saying, "I pray that all is well with you and that your physical body is as healthy as your spiritual character." Study the text to know that he makes this statement because word is spread abroad about the integrity of Gaius and his devotion to walking in the truth. I am not suggesting we should not pray for one another's financial success, but that financial success should not be just to prosper you, but to share it with others who are less fortunate than you. My point is we should not use this Scripture to suggest that the writer is wishing him to have super riches above all else. John didn't say it like that, so if that's what you desire for people, then let that be your personal exhortation, but don't manipulate the Scripture to support what you may desire.

God does not bless us just for us; He blesses us to be a blessing to others.

The problem trend I've witnessed is one that gets people amped up about potential financial prosperity by naming it and claiming it. It is a strategy used through biblical ignorance in some cases, but it's an intentional strategy to justify one's own explanation for their personal ill gained wealth in other cases. God is not sanctioning some of these preaching methods for getting money. Honestly gained wealth is acquired through hard work and through the use of your gifts and talents. The purest example of that wealth is when you use it to help poor people who need help from those who have been blessed to be wealthy. God does not bless us just for us;

He blesses us to be a blessing to others. To do anything other than that is to be foolish—look at the parable of the Rich Fool who Jesus taught us about. This parable is Jesus' reflection and discourse on the foolishness of attaching too much emphasis on financial wealth:

> And he spake a parable unto them, saying, "The ground of a certain rich man brought forth plentifully:" And he thought within himself, saying, "What shall I do, because I have no room where to bestow my fruits?" And he said, "This will I do: I will pull down my barns, and build greater; and there will I bestow all my fruits and my goods. And I will say to my soul, Soul, thou hast much goods laid up for many years; take thine ease, eat, drink, and be merry." But God said unto him, "Thou fool, this night thy soul shall be required of thee: then whose shall those things be, which thou hast provided? So is he that layeth up treasure for himself, and is not rich toward God." — Luke 12:16–21, KJV

Notice that this man was not called foolish because he was rich, lazy and slothful. He was called foolish because he did not use his wealth in a way that would benefit others. He was also called foolish because he thought he was the reason for his wealth instead of God. Listen to him so loosely using the words *I* and *My* as though he sent the rain and the sunshine that caused his crops to grow. When we feel that we deserve to keep everything that we earn for ourselves and not share it with others, we are making those decisions at the risk of excluding God as being the person who made it happen. Everything good that I have, I believe that God made it happen. And for that reason alone, I try to give as much to other people who are in need. This idea of sowing into rich people because it helps you to get rich is a lie and a scam to manipulate people. Jesus laid out a true principle regarding his life by saying that the well do not need a physician, but the sick do. He came to help those who had spiritual needs, physical needs, and material needs. He did not come just to help those who had more than what they needed. He came to help and to heal the poor and to heal the broken hearted.

> And after these things he went forth, and saw a publican, named Levi, sitting at the receipt of custom: and he said unto him, "Follow me." And he left all, rose up, and followed him. And Levi made him a great feast in

> his own house: and there was a great company of publicans and of others that sat down with them. But their scribes and Pharisees murmured against his disciples, saying, "Why do ye eat and drink with publicans and sinners?" And Jesus answering said unto them, "They that are whole need not a physician; but they that are sick. I came not to call the righteous, but sinners to repentance." — Luke 5:27–32

Throughout the Scriptures, Jesus did not give food to the greedy, but to the needy; the miracle of the five loaves and two fish shows us that. As it relates to the rich, he constantly warned his disciples to be careful how they gave heart and soul to the riches of this world. Buying cars and planes and houses for people who can afford them is not acting in the wisdom and the Spirit of Christ and his teachings. I know many preachers who will read this and say, "It's my money, and I can do with it what I choose." I respond by saying you are an offender of the Gospel and should not be preaching because you have perverted the very Gospel that you preach and are walking in sin. If you are a pastor and you get wealthy from being one, then you need to be helping the poor people in your church, not constantly taking from them. That is wrong on any day and if you say you have the Holy Spirt in you, then my question is why is it that many of you don't hear him tell you these things?

> A person who gets ahead by oppressing the poor or by showering gifts on the rich will end in poverty. — Proverbs 22:16, NLT

> He said also to the man who had invited him, "When you give a dinner or a banquet, do not invite your friends or your brothers or your relatives or rich neighbors, lest they also invite you in return and you be repaid. But when you give a feast, invite the poor, the crippled, the lame, the blind, and you will be blessed, because they cannot repay you. For you will be repaid at the resurrection of the just." — Luke 14:12–14, ESV

> The blessings of the Lord makes a person rich, and he adds no sorrow with it. — Proverbs 10:22, NLT

When we believers walk in the standards of God and labor for the advancement of the Kingdom of God and His people, He will bless the works of our hands. You can't just make an offering in the church bucket and receive those blessings; it takes effort and energy on your part. God will increase you. I believe that. He will bless your business, and you won't be stressed about it. Sorrow does not await those who are willing to sow in labor and time and service, but peace and godly prosperity will abound in your life. It's not naming it and claiming it. It's walking and working it. The following Scripture is a principle of reference to what Solomon is saying in the aforementioned scripture:

> Then Isaac sowed in that land, and received in the same year an hundredfold: and the Lord blessed him. And the man waxed great, and went forward, and grew until he became very great: For he had possession of flocks, and possession of herds, and great store of servants: and the Philistines envied him. — Genesis 26:12–14, KJV

Notice the text says Isaac sowed in that land. The operative phrase is *that land* because that land was famine land. There was no natural possibility that land could produce anything good, but Isaac followed the ways of his father Abraham by not going to Egypt for government help. He chose to trust God, and he stayed where God sent him. So what did he sow? He sowed seeds, labor and hard work, and he sowed something far greater; he sowed his obedience to God in tough times. As a result, God blessed him with riches and added no sorrow to it. Nothing had to be manipulated, stolen, or hustled. God is the one who will make it happen for you. There's so much to this story. You should read it in its entirety.

> **If you are a pastor and you get wealthy from being one, then you need to be helping the poor people in your church, not constantly taking from them.**

Another Scripture that is often used out of context to suggest some kind of effortless access to wealth is **"The wealth of the wicked is laid up for the just."** This is not all of what this Scriptures says in Proverbs 13:22. People quote and teach this Scripture as if there is some ungodly person who's going to leave people his or her money. Here is what that Scripture says in its entirety:

RICH SHEPHERD, POOR SHEEP

> Good people leave an inheritance to their grandchildren, but the sinner's wealth is laid up for the righteous.
> — Proverbs 13:22, NLT

So what exactly is the wisdom of Solomon here? People who properly handle the affairs of their estate would ensure that before they die, their children and their grandchildren are provided for properly. They leave a will because they are concerned about the perpetuation of generations to come. Now an ungodly, foolish and selfish man will live his life without regard for anyone but himself. He will die without making those provisions, and God, in his wise providence, will see to it that some righteous person enjoys those benefits. It is my personal assumption that even foolish and ungodly persons can have godly relatives who they give or leave nothing for, and they could be the ones who ends up with the estate.

> Evil people may have piles of money and may store away mounds of clothing. But the righteous will wear that clothing, and the innocent will divide that money.
> — Job 27:16–17, NLT

It is a truth that God favors His people who live their lives for Him, but He does not expect them to be depending on something that someone may leave them as an inheritance. We all must strive to work at using our gifts that God gives us that could cause us to experience financial prosperity. I personally have always seen the wealth of the wicked as the wisdom and will of the wicked rich to know how to use their business acumen to gain wealth. A lot of believers, as well as non-believers, fall prey to these get-rich-quick schemes due to their attempt to avoid processes that mandate hard work, sweat and patience. God will always direct your path in a way that complements the efforts you make in your attempt to prosper for the sake of righteousness. Your desire must be for more than just personal prosperity that's designed to enrich only you and yours; you must be willing to bless the less fortunate.

> If ye shall ask any thing in my name, I will do it.
> — John 14:14, KJV

Many people quote this Scripture with the implication that *any thing* means everything. They conclude that all you have to do is tag it "In Jesus' Name." This is not true in the context that many people use it. Some people see this as a mechanism that will give them whatever they want.

When Jesus makes this statement, it is to be noted that you must include the preceding verses:

> Jesus saith unto him, "I am the way, the truth, and the life: no man cometh unto the Father, but by me. If ye had known me, ye should have known my Father also: and from henceforth ye know him, and have seen him." Philip saith unto him, "Lord, show us the Father, and it sufficeth us." Jesus saith unto him, "Have I been so long time with you, and yet hast thou not known me, Philip? He that hath seen me hath seen the Father; and how sayest thou then, Show us the Father? Believest thou not that I am in the Father, and the Father in me? The words that I speak unto you I speak not of myself: but the Father that dwelleth in me, he doeth the works. Believe me that I am in the Father, and the Father in me: or else believe me for the very works' sake. Verily, verily, I say unto you, 'He that believeth on me, the works that I do shall he do also; and greater works than these shall he do; because I go unto my Father. And whatsoever ye shall ask in my name, that will I do, that the Father may be glorified in the Son. If ye shall ask any thing in my name, I will do it.'" — John 14:6–14, KJV

When you study this text within the context of how Jesus spoke it, you will see the specificity of his discourse with the disciples. Phillip spoke in a way that revealed that he and the disciples had not grasped the understanding that Son of God means equal with God. They requested that Jesus show them the Father when, in actuality, he was the Father revealed through the Son. Jesus was teaching them the truth that any and all access to the Father came through him. He's teaching them principles that must be applied once he has completed his mission on earth and had gone to take his seat at the right hand of the Father. Jesus is not in any way teaching a principle that says you can get anything from God if you use his name. He is speaking more on spiritual connections and not material or natural and fleshly consumptions. Also note that when he says "greater works ye shall do," he's not talking about having greater things or doing things he could not do. Jesus was not God while he's having this dialogue. His omni attributes are not being used because he emptied himself of those deities to become human. The greater works will happen for us on earth because he has gone to the Father and is interceding on our behalf, plus he will send the Holy Spirit to dwell within believers, giving them power to function with a supernatural empowerment. This power is giving to us to walk in love and obedience to the will of God for our lives. This is not power to get stuff in a material sense. The material stuff will come as we become good stewards of that which he commissions us to do. Jesus is talking about greater ministry works, not greater material stuff.

> For ye know the grace of our Lord Jesus Christ, that, though he was rich, yet for your sakes he became poor, that ye through his poverty might be rich. — 2 Corinthians 8:9, KJV

This is another of those Scriptures in which the words *poor*, *poverty* and *rich* are not referring to financial riches as the effect of the cause. Paul is encouraging and giving thanks to those who are contributing to a cause to help others. It has nothing to do with Jesus dying to poverty, so you and I can be rich. The spiritual riches that God offers are much greater than financial riches. It is heresy to misinterpret Scriptures by substituting the true definition of words to promote a prosperity message. Like I said before, if this were true, then all believers would be financially rich, not just the ones who preach and teach it.

Now read the rest of the conversation of the letter, so you can get the truth of what's being relayed by the Apostle Paul.

> "You know the generous grace of our Lord Jesus Christ. Though he was rich, yet for your sakes he became poor, so that by his poverty he could make you rich. Here is my advice: It would be good for you to finish what you started a year ago. Last year you were the first who wanted to give, and you were the first to begin doing it. Now you should finish what you started. Let the eagerness you showed in the beginning be matched now by your giving. Give in proportion to what you have. Whatever you give is acceptable if you give it eagerly. And give according to what you have, not what you don't have. Of course, I don't mean your giving should make life easy for others and hard for yourselves. I only mean that there should be some equality. Right now you have plenty and can help those who are in need. Later, they

will have plenty and can share with you when you need it. In this way, things will be equal. As the Scriptures say, "Those who gathered a lot had nothing left over, and those who gathered only a little had enough." — 2 Corinthians 8:9–15 NLT

To conclude, let me reiterate the spiritual integrity of the scriptural text that should always accompany what we preach and teach. So many false doctrines in the Church arise not of themselves but through the perpetual perversion of manipulated agendas that compromise truth with corrupt teachings. I take the Scriptures seriously because I take God seriously and the learning of his sheep seriously. If the Bible didn't mean it, then don't you make it a mastery of your teachings. God bless those of you who follow homiletic and hermeneutic integrity without compromise.

CHAPTER TEN

WHO'S COVERING YOU? THE ACCOUNTABILITY IN COLLEGIALITY

Much is being taught regarding the relationship between apostolic fathers and their sons. Unfortunately, there is a shallowness of spiritual insight that plagues the ecclesiastical peripheries of the apostolic vision and purpose. As I sit in focused writing, giving meditational discipline and careful discernment to the voice of God, I feel provoked to give detailed attention and description to the dictates I am hearing from the Holy Spirit. I have observed over the years a misguided representation of true fatherhood on so many levels that the result is that a new reformation of true apostolic fathering must take front and center stage on the landscape of apostolic connection, correction and covering. Because of my desire to fulfill my every God-ordained vision, I've made this area of my apostolic mantle a mandated priority to my forward movement. I challenge every apostle, prophet, evangelist, pastor and teacher who's giving oversight to people in any capacity to get a true spiritual covering for the purpose of accountability. Please note that when I use the term *sons*, I am also referencing daughters as well. The term *son* is in the neutral tense, except where a Scripture is inserted and is in that case referencing males. I do believe that women have a place and call in ministry.

The Principle of Accountability

To be accountable is the willingness to obligate yourself to accepting responsibility for that which you have committed yourself to. It is the integrity of your character to live your life under the transparent view of persons whom you give permission to judge your behavior. In various professions, colleagues who are of the same or similar career specificity share a common and cooperative bond and relationship of collegiality. Proverbs 27:17 says, **"As iron sharpens iron, so a friend sharpens a friend"** NLT. I tend to believe that a part of the problem in the Church Body, from the pulpit to the pew, is that many people appear to have responsibilities in ministry, but no consistent checking for accountability. Usually, by the time a decision is made that determines an action of accountability, things may have either spun way out of control or conformed, and comfort patterns of behaviors may have formed, and resistance and rebellion become the response. Many people in leadership positions feel as though they are above and beyond being accountable. This happens because they feel that their intelligence and integrity are being questioned. Any person who is willing to work as a hire or volunteer for a company and resists accountability gets his or her integrity of character questioned immediately. People who always resist help and or evaluations are usually protecting something they are trying to keep hidden.

> **Many people in leadership positions feel as though they are above and beyond being accountable. This happens because they feel that their intelligence and integrity are being questioned.**

In this chapter, my focus and goal are to help pastors understand the importance of having someone or certain people in their lives to cover them and to keep them accountable to moral and ethical standards. It is dangerous to be a leader of people and the only voice you are listening to for counsel and brainstorming is your own. This is often the biggest sign of insecurity and an arrogant and egocentric perspective of life. My response to people who themselves say that can't nobody tell me nothing, I say that I can tell because it appears you are operating on a limited amount of competent fueled substance of the brain. When we refuse to surround ourselves with competent people, where collegiality can be embraced and shared, we are preventing ourselves from becoming exceptional leaders. The idea of accountability partners is no new age idea; it is a long-standing common denominator that exists in most if not all areas of service and leadership professionals. It is not subservient to put yourself under a form of personal checks and balances, but it is self-serving not to employ other wisdom inflections. In life, you not only need people who you can talk to and listen to you. But it is refreshing and rehabilitative to have people who can talk to you and whom you can listen to. Your view of life and certain ideologies of thinking are not the only view there is. You must be willing to see things, at times, through the lens of opposing or opposite views.

Allow me to give some biblical perspective and application to this discussion on covering and accountability. I believe that who is covering you is more important than who you are covering, simply because it shows how serious you take being responsible to others as much as you expect others to be responsible to you. You just can't go around serving what you don't eat, preaching what you don't practice, and teaching what you don't believe. Let me introduce you to my apostolic covering. His name is Dr. John Testola; he is a true apostolic father to me, and he walks in true apostolic integrity, maturity and gift. He is a reformer, transitioning nations and churches to follow the principles of the Kingdom of God. He is an author of more than one hundred and fifty books and leads a structured ministry in the Bronx, New York.

> **It is not subservient to put yourself under a form of personal checks and balances, but it is self-serving not to employ other wisdom inflections.**

I am submitted to his authority and guidance. And where discipline is needed, he gives it and I accept it. Spiritual fathers are not called to open doors of opportunities for their sons as much as they are called to open windows of understanding and revelation knowledge that in itself will open doors of opportunities for advancement. Where development is needed, he gives it to me, and I embrace every dimension of the process. I do not allow him to think for me, but I allow him to think with me, which is how it should be. You can't grow under someone who is a dictator in your life. They must be a director, using their wisdom and knowledge to bring out what God has placed within you. I honor him by supporting his ministry and giving to him as I am led in my heart to do and at the leading of the Holy Spirit. Every pastor needs a covering!

The Principle and Purpose of the Apostolic Covering

The principle of a thing is the standard idea that governs the functioning of that thing. It is the comprehensive and fundamental doctrine or assumption of a thing. When I speak of the apostolic covering, I am not talking denominational jargon. I am referencing spiritual governing authority. I believe that God has given certain people who are called of him and submitted to him access to function at a specific level of authority. Now this doesn't make them better than anyone else. They just have a different level of responsibility and protocol. The purpose in having an apostolic covering is to have a matured person with a proven ministry to serve in a mentoring capacity in your life. Many also call this kind of person a spiritual father or spiritual covering. This in no way places this person above God who called you. The purpose is to have some living human being whose wisdom is beyond yours who can walk with you through your life process.

The Word of God speaks to this principle of covering and accountability in both Old and New Testament Scriptures. The Apostle Paul was a great apostolic father in the faith of our Lord Jesus Christ. He expresses his fatherly love and leadership to his children in the Gospel:

> I write not these things to shame you, but to admonish you as my beloved children. For though ye have ten thousand tutors in Christ, yet have ye not many fathers; for in Christ Jesus I begat you through the gospel. I beseech you therefore, be ye imitators of me. For this cause have I sent unto you Timothy, who is my beloved and faithful child in the Lord, who shall put you in remembrance of my ways which are in Christ, even as I teach everywhere in every church. — 1 Corinthians 4:14–17, ASV

Paul is drawing a clear distinction between the many teachers who believers will have in their lifetime, but the missing element needed to push people into deeper levels of spiritual maturity is fatherhood. Paul has a clear understanding that spiritual fatherhood has become his ministry, but it was his by stewardship not ownership. Being a spiritual father is never a license of ownership over another minister or ministry. We are servants and stewards, no matter what level of ministry we are chosen to function in. Many leaders fall prey to a controlling and manipulative spirit as they seek to dominate and dictate the course of other people's lives. Notice also that Paul is setting the example as a father by instructing his followers to imitate not him the person, but him the one who is imitating Christ. People should never be driven to be like us, but to be like the Christ whom we exhibit, and any patterns that don't reflect Christ should be rejected.

In the New Testament, especially with the Apostle Paul, we see the significance of the father-son relationship in its purest form. Paul was a role model of what I believe is a pattern to follow for those who consider themselves spiritual fathers to other men and women of God and ministries. In dealing with the various churches, Paul never served in the role of a pastor, but in the role of an apostolic father. Many today do not believe in the gift of the apostle, but I believe that all the gifts in Ephesians chapter four are essential to the maturation of the saints. Even though Paul was not one of the twelve original apostles, neither was Barnabas, but according to Acts 14:14, they both functioned as apostolic men. In this book, I am not trying to argue a difference of biblical views, but I am attempting to lay out a foundation that will help get the Church of today past this stagnation of religious ideologies and denominational discords that are not biblical but are present in today's religious circles. Pastors need fathers, and churches need pastors who are being fathered by true apostolic men who have had an encounter with God and have ministries and lives that give proof to their callings. We are in a divisional war of religion verses righteousness, humanistic ideologies and doctrinal discords against strategic principalities and powers that are ruling in our communities and cities. We have egocentric leaders who have inserted their agendas for personal prominence ahead of the agenda and mission of the Church to win the world to God. Fathers are absent at home and in the Church. Fathers are in prisons that are financial investment institutions for the rich. There are spiritual fathers who are in prison to a watered-down theology and a wealth-infused message that does not provide prosperity for the poor. You have rich spiritual fathers with poor spiritual sons. We need some correction in the Body of Christ.

Pastors need fathers, and churches need pastors who are being fathered by true apostolic men who have had an encounter with God and have ministries and lives that give proof to their callings.

Now let me move past that argument and move into a teaching that portrays the life of a prominent prophetic father and son relationship, Elijah and Elisha. The narratives that I share here will give us an Old Testament view of the ministry connection and spiritual connection between these two prophets. I will begin sharing with you how Elijah seeks out Elisha and show how that connection is made between the two of them.

> "So Elijah went and found Elisha son of Shaphat plowing a field. There were twelve teams of oxen in the field, and Elisha was plowing with the twelfth team. Elijah went over to him and threw his cloak across his shoulders and then walked away. Elisha left the oxen standing there, ran after Elijah, and said to him, "First let me go and kiss my father and mother good-bye, and then I will go with you!" Elijah replied, "Go on back, but think about what I have done to you." So Elisha returned to his oxen and slaughtered them. He used the wood from the plow to build a fire to roast their flesh. He passed around the meat to the townspeople, and they all ate. Then he went with Elijah as his assistant." — 1 Kings 19:19–21, NLT

We must notice some interesting dynamics to this connection. Elijah had hit a an emotional and psychological low in his life. After his encounter with Ahab and Jezebel due to the Mount Carmel showdown between Jehovah God and the god Baal along with the prophets of Baal who sat at Jezebel's command. He is now a fugitive on the run and becomes totally overwhelmed to the point of a meltdown and near breakdown. After Elijah's meltdown, God intervenes and reminds him that he's not the only prophet He has, but is one of many. So now God is preparing him for his transition, and He tells Elijah to seek out Elisha who will become his helper and replacement. The Bible says clearly that Elijah seeks him out and finds him, and when he passes Elisha, he throws his mantle over him. The mantle was a cloak-like garment that prophets wore. It symbolizes the prophet's authority and responsibility. Once he throws it over him, Elijah keeps walking, and Elisha runs after him, but Elijah tells him to go and think about what I have done to you. There is a thought process to every new shift in our lives and whenever we are called to do something. Discernment and the understanding of directions and expectations must be a part of the equation of thought. Elijah was impressing upon Elisha to give serious thought to what he was about to experience.

Elisha goes and does exactly that, and he prepares roasted oxen and gives them to the town's people. He then begins to pursue after Elijah and assist him. Please note that three things happen in this connection between Elijah and Elisha that should serve as a type of pattern for spiritual fathers and their spiritual sons.

1. **God Chose Elisha for Elijah:** No matter what the case may be, when it comes to spiritual matters regarding appointments and appointees and assignments and assignees, God should be the one who guides our selection of individuals to serve us or the ministries we give oversight to. Every person who desires your covering is not designed for your covering, and some people don't deserve your covering because some want only to be connected to your success and not committingly submitted to your service as a spiritual leader. How many spiritual sons you have is not as important as how many you can serve effectively and help to mature.

2. **Elijah Charged and Challenged Elisha's Will:** It is my belief that hasty decisions without hard inflection and reflection is a hinderance to making a good decision. Every call can wait a response because when you respond to that call, you must bring all that you are into it. The father-son connection is one of all things good and bad within the persons connected. No one brings perfection of character to the table, but maturity of character and conduct. Elisha was challenged to think about the charge that was being laid upon him before he followed Elijah.

3. **Elisha Chased and Pursued Elijah:** The chase and pursuit of one who you believe to be someone whom you are called to is not a demeaning of your character. I would like to say emphatically that it is a testament of your sincerity and seriousness. Sons always pursue their fathers while fathers protect and parent their sons. The purpose of the pursuit is to capture what's in the chosen father that is connected to your purpose and destiny. Before you can ever lock into what's in your spiritual father, you must latch on to him. It's like the principle of the umbilical cord, which is the cord that sends life nutrients to the fetus, causing it to grow. Ultimately, after a period of required months, and the baby is birthed out of the uterus into the world, it is cut from the umbilical cord, but it's not cut from the mother. Now, not only

can the mother feed the baby, but also other selected persons can help in the future growth feeding and process. Spiritual fathers help to establish spiritually healthly foundations for their sons, so they can have the right influences from which to draw from as they begin to build their lives toward their purpose and destiny.

Now that Elisha has connected to Elijah in 1 Kings chapter nineteen, lets move into chapter two of 2 Kings and discover the progression of that relationship. In the Old Testament book of 2Kings 2:9–13, we find the story of the transference of prophetic power and leadership from the prophet Elijah to his son, the prophet Elisha. It is here also that we see the father-son connection between the two prophetic giants in the faith. You should also notice that fifty other prophetic sons were being mentored by Elijah as seen in 2 Kings 2:5, but they did not follow Elijah to the end as Elisha did. To me, their persistence and pursuit appear to have reached its limit or uncertainty, but Elisha was after something deeper from his father in the Lord. Consider this biblical narrative:

> And it came to pass, when they were gone over, that Elijah said unto Elisha, "Ask what I shall do for thee, before I am taken from thee." And Elisha said, "I pray thee, let a double portion of thy spirit be upon me." And he said, "Thou hast asked a hard thing: nevertheless, if thou see me when I am taken from thee, it shall be so unto thee; but if not, it shall not be so." And it came to pass, as they still went on, and talked, that, behold, there appeared a chariot of fire, and horses of fire, which parted them both asunder; and Elijah went up by a whirlwind into heaven.
>
> And Elisha saw it, and he cried, "My father, my father, the chariots of Israel and the horsemen thereof!" And he saw him no more: and he took hold of his own clothes, and rent them in two pieces. He took up also the mantle of Elijah that fell from him, and went back, and stood by the bank of the Jordan. — 2 Kings 2:9–13, ASV

1. **Spiritual Connections are for the Cause of Spiritual Conclusions:** There are some disparities in some of the father-son connections that we see in today's ministry circles. The functioning of some of these relationships has become so off-base until it is,

at times, embarrassing. Instead of the main thrust of the relationship being on spiritual enrichment, the spirit of materialism and style has become the copy-cat attraction. Young preachers are pursuing certain men of God because of their iconic status and charismatic style and fashion statements. There appears to be no hunger for spiritual depth or scriptural substance. Today, many are chasing the wrong thing and, unfortunately, too many spiritual fathers are offering the wrong things. Many stories and rumors of unhealthy relationships have led to perverted seductions that are demonic and out of the bounds of godly parenting. It's bad when the relationship with the spiritual father is more revered than the relationship with our heavenly Father. When Elisha was asked by Elijah what he wanted of him, Elisha did not request anything material. He asked for a double portion of his father's spirit to be upon him. He wanted to function in the same power of influence in which he saw his spiritual father function, except he wanted a double portion. That should always be the desire of the son, to exceed the works of the father, not in competition but as a good steward who credits himself by increasing and enhancing that which is given to him. Elisha was more interested in the prophetic work of his father. He had no interest in any forms of material prosperity and wealth. Elijah told Elisha that the thing he asked for was difficult, but he didn't tell him it was impossible—that it was just conditional. He was told by Elijah that he had to be with him when he completed his journey and was carried away by the chariot of fire. True fathers don't leave their sons. They are taken away from them by divine interventions. Sons stay with their fathers for life until there is a divine intervention that interrupts the connection. I don't believe that you swap fathers every so many years or until the next popular preacher comes along. I, like the Apostle Paul, believe we have many teachers who influence our lives, but I don't believe we have many fathers.

2. **Spiritual Connections are Confirmed by a Personal Commitment:** Most noticeable to me in this narrative is that Elisha never swayed or strayed in his commitment to Elijah. He stayed with him, and they continued to walk together and share conversation and dialogue. In a true spiritual connection, their conversation and communication was between both father and son. No records document what their conversations were, but

based on my personal relationship with my natural sons, I can only imagine that not only was Elijah pouring into Elisha, but I'm sure Elijah gleaned insights from his son as well. Fathers must be willing to listen and trust their children's discernment and, at times, their alternative directions. There should never exist a negative competition of power struggling egocentricity and jealousy between a father and his children. It should be to the delight of the father to hear and watch the maturation of his sons to the point where the son can feel comfortable in sharing his views with his father. Fathers must accept the counsel of their sons and not create a perverted loyalty that does not allow room for their sons to question or constructively confront them when they have questions. I live by the principle that people who you can't ask questions to are people you shouldn't follow. Another important principle to consider in the father-son connection is the understanding of both parties' role and responsibility. Fathers are called to build and develop the value systems of their sons while sons bear and build their father's vision. God and Jesus is a prime example of this model. Jesus said his will was to do the will of his Father. He carried out God's vision for the redemption of man, by giving his life for mankind. He did this repeatedly throughout his life, and it brought pleasure to his Father. Elisha remained steadfast with his father and when the time of transitioning occurred, Elijah was taken away and when he was being taken away, Elisha shouted and cried, "My father, my father, the chariots of Israel and the horsemen thereof!" And he saw him no more. Please note that when Elijah went up into the heavens, he left his spiritual mantle of authority and inheritance for his son, and he left it within his reach. He didn't have to struggle to get it. His father made it easy for him to catch it because his son followed the mandate to the end.

How beautiful the stories of the Bible are, and this one in general. The record is that Elisha, upon receiving his father's mantle, began immediately to operate in the spirit that was upon his father. I tell the thirty-plus ministers where I serve as servant leader that if they watch me, they'll catch me and understand how to walk with me. You can't stay absent and understand the assignment and inherit the mantle.

Now, Elisha begins a whole new chapter in his life, and there still remains some revelational insight to be gained as we take a brief look at an episode in Elisha's life that gives us further understanding of the connection between the father and son relationship.

PRINCIPLES FOR CULTIVATING HEALTHY FATHER AND SON RELATIONSHIPS: THE ELISHA PROPHETIC DISCOURSE

> One day the group of prophets came to Elisha and told him, "As you can see, this place where we meet with you is too small. Let's go down to the Jordan River, where there are plenty of logs. There we can build a new place for us to meet." "All right," he told them, "go ahead." "Please come with us," someone suggested. "I will," he said. So he went with them. When they arrived at the Jordan, they began cutting down trees. But as one of them was cutting a tree, his ax head fell into the river. "Oh, sir!" he cried. "It was a borrowed ax!" "Where did it fall?" the man of God asked. When he showed him the place, Elisha cut a stick and threw it into the water at that spot. Then the ax head floated to the surface. "Grab it," Elisha said. And the man reached out and grabbed it. — 2 Kings 6:1-7, NLT

Elisha is mentoring several of his prophetic sons and it is obvious there is growth occurring during this mentorship because they came with a vision idea and recommendation to relocate the school of prophetic ministry due to the need of more space to accommodate the expansion and growth.

Principle One: It is a wonderful thing when spiritual sons are able to submit vision to their fathers, so they can support them and so their sons can develop being independent thinkers.

Spiritual fathers are called to give their children foundation, but their children must be allowed to build their own structures. As I stated before, spiritual fathers are not called to think for their spiritual sons but to think with them. Some spiritual fathers have the idea they need to be the ears that hear God for their sons; however, I think that's quite out of bounds and out of order and can be a hindrance to the spiritual development of the sons. You shouldn't be giving them the messages they preach. It's one thing to give them a focus idea to concentrate on, but let them seek

God for the details of the message. Remember, you're not their master, but their mentor and guide. They have a responsibility to God first and then to you. Every Sunday at my church, I designate a different minister to bring a five-minute inspirational message. I don't tell them what to preach, but I designate how much time they have to present that message. By doing this, they develop a good discipline for time, content, and delivery. I make it a concerted effort to be sitting front and center to hear them and to encourage them, especially the ones who I haven't yet heard in a public setting. I also intentionally embrace them once they finish as a source of affirmation.

Principle Two: Affirmation is a great accompaniment to the aspirations, ambitions, and inspiration of your spiritual sons.

Notice in the text that one of the young prophets informed Elisha of their going to the Jordan River because the resource of lumber was more sufficient than where they were. The young prophet asked Elisha to accompany them there. Elisha, however, stated they should go ahead without him. However, the young prophet pleaded with him to go with them. That was a great moment in that text because it had some true exposure of need that these and many other sons have. They wanted their father to be on the set and in their sight, even though they didn't want him to do the work. Fathers, your sons are excited when you come around while they are working because your presence is their affirmation. Don't just use them when it benefits you; make yourself available to them because it benefits them. Elisha did accordingly

> **Spiritual fathers are called to give their children foundation, but their children must be allowed to build their own structures.**

and went with them because that's what true fathers do. Unfortunately, we have seen the reduction of the value of spiritual sons drop down to opening doors, running errands, carrying brief cases and Bibles. We have to drop this celebrity status mentality because it is not the model we see portrayed in Scripture. These are your sons, not your slaves, and they have so much more to offer in ministry than to cater to your iconic self-centeredness and need to feel significant. Get over it or get out because if this is the kind of covering you are, then you are contaminated and should be isolated and quarantined to yourself.

Principle Three: Give them opportunity to do things that will challenge their creativity.

The trees in this text were not negative obstructions or obstacles to the vision at hand. They were resources and opportunities of challenges that were necessary for the purpose of the vision. Every tree you face in your life has something in it that can help you to advance. You have to be willing to hit them, even using the resources of other covenant relationships when necessary. If things break around you during the process, God has a way of working those things out. Besides, He works great in broken situations and with broken pieces. Being a good ministry father mandates you to let your sons take a swing at life and vision. You are always there to help them if the need arises. And trust me, the need always arises. I believe that is so much better for your sons—and even you—to break something that's useful while trying to do something that is significant and progressive. It's better than being lazy of vision and progressive thinking. Remember, reparation is a resource of responsibility that is given to every spiritual leader for the purpose of restoring and realigning our sons and daughters when they hit and miss or hit and break.

Principle Four: It's important to know where the son's role ends and where the father's role begins.

When the young prophet broke and lost a borrowed ax head while building onto his father's vision, he went straight to his man of God for a resolve to a problem that emotionally disturbed him. The ministry of a spiritual father is to always know how to help their sons find the things they lose to unexpected circumstances. I have witnessed situations in which ministry sons have fallen to scandal and personal improprieties that are common to human nature. In those situations, I've seen so called spiritual fathers run for the nearest fire escape, abandoning their sons in order to protect their own reputations. People in general need us when they fall and when they fail; we can't just claim them when they're good and cast them away when they mess up. The Apostle Paul instructs us:

> **The ministry of a spiritual father is to always know how to help their sons find the things they lose to unexpected circumstances.**

> Brethren if a man be overtaken in a fault, ye which are spiritual, restore such an one in the spirit of meekness; considering thyself, lest thou also be tempted. — Galatians 6:1

As a spiritual father, you owe it to those you cover to stand by them in every situation, giving them counsel that they must adhere to. If they do not adhere to that counsel, you must release them to their disobedience. After a very short period, however, you must reach back out to them for restoration, lest they they become totally lost. This principle is recorded in 1 Corinthians 5:5, where Paul writes, **"To deliver such an one unto satan for the destruction of the flesh, that the spirit may be saved in the day of the Lord Jesus"** KJV. However, the follow up for restoration is recorded in 2 Corinthians:

> I am not overstating it when I say that the man who caused all the trouble hurt you all more than he hurt me. Most of you opposed him, and that was punishment enough. Now however, it is time to forgive and comfort him. Otherwise he may be overcome by discouragement. So I urge you now to reaffirm your love for him. — 2 Corinthians 2:5–8, NLT

During this time of separation, you should be making intercession for them that the Holy Spirit may discipline them and bring them to a place of conviction and correction. Our sons need our loyalty just as much as we need their loyalty and, in most cases, require their loyalty. Elisha did not buckle; he just said take me to the place where you lost it. Most people know when they've messed up and where they messed up, so be willing to walk those paths with them in love.

Principle Five: A true spiritual father knows how to make his son's ax head float:

The head of an ax is its sharpest and most needed part. Without it, it has and serves no purpose. Elisha did not panic when the young prophet came to him with a challenge. He asked him to show him exactly where he dropped it. Then he used a piece of what the young man was working against to revive what he thought he lost. The power of a spiritual father lies within his ability to help his children reclaim what they feel they've lost and can't recover while trying to do a good thing. Fathers have to know how to make their children's ax heads float. When someone is spiritually connected to us and is in covenant with us, God gives us specific wisdom and insight to minister to him or her in ways that no other person can. Remember, we reap not only what we sow, but we also reap where we sow. Sons who are committed to us in service as unto the Lord have seed in us and should ultimately reap from the anointing that God has on our lives. We possess the anointing to help them see what they can't see, seek what they can't find, and survive the things they feel they have to succumb to. There is protection in connection, especially when that connection is a God-ordained one.

Principle Six: Spiritual fathers are called to point out their son's losses, not recover losses for them.

Elisha made the young prophet's ax head float, but the young prophet had to retrieve it once it was in sight. That's what you call taking responsibility by participating in your own recovery. This gave the young prophet a stewardship of responsibility for doing what's necessary to find what he lost because it wasn't his to lose but his only to use. By instructing him to reach into the water to retrieve it once it floated to the top, he now has an ownership responsibility, and he learns to reach into situations that were a potential obstacle to him at first. Fathers have a unique joy and stake in the lives of their sons. You get to help them climb high and reach deep, never running from the challenges that face them. By Elisha being there with his sons, it created an environment of hope in the midst of what could've been a hopeless situation had he not been there or had his son not felt the confidence to go to his father once he had made an unintentional mistake. What a great lesson of revelation we can learn from this biblical narrative.

Fathers have a unique joy and stake in the lives of their sons. You get to help them climb high and reach deep, never running from the challenges that face them.

When choosing someone as a covering, it is important that you do so prayerfully and in the wisdom of God. There are so many manipulating opportunists on both sides of this spectrum, so you must do so in great caution. It is such an honor of integrity when you have someone in your life to hold you accountable; I can't say that enough. Don't be a lone ranger, walking through this life of ministry by yourself. Make sure you are truly connected to that person by the Spirit and nothing else.

Fathers, don't determine who your sons should be by the size of their church or by their financial position, but by the guidance of the Holy Spirit, just like Elijah chose Elisha. Pastors, the people who follow you will respect and trust you more when they see you submitted to someone else. Please embrace the things you've read here and allow these truths to set you free into a more healthy spiritual journey. Every shepherd covering God's sheep needs the insight of a matured and experienced leader. I pray that the information here has helped you to see clearer through the fog of failed representation of the father-son connection. The rip off and the set up are bigger than many of us could ever imagine or would ever admit. This is why you must remain accountable to a true covering and watch God do incredible things in your life and ministry.

EPILOGUE
IT'S TIME TO GO ANOTHER WAY –
THE CALL TO RESTORATION

When I began to understand the directives I was given by the Holy Spirit to write this book, I knew that every word and principle had to have a purpose. As I stated in the introduction, this book was not written to be a tabloid of gossip or attacks on any specific person's character. I wanted to provide something wholesome and edifying to the world at large, so the integrity of the Gospel could be restored and reclaimed by those who have been bruised and battered by the unfortunate fallacies of the local church and pastor. I did not want to pen a document filled with observations with no solutions, questions with no answers, criticisms with no correction. I believe I have, by the grace of God and to the best of my current ability, done just that. However, I want to close by suggesting to a broad spectrum of the Body of Christ the importance of a change of direction.

IT'S TIME FOR US TO GO ANOTHER WAY

We have experienced a major eclipse of spiritual power from the human tendencies of mankind. The true son has, in some ways, been blocked by the ways and behaviors of men who have overrated themselves and, in so many ways, overshadowed the main character Jesus who is never to become lost within entities that claim to be His Church. We must call for restoration, cry for revival, create a new reformation ideology that mimics the Kingdom of God it its purest sense. We must be willing to combat against rebellion and religious laced and based theology that has no power that propel men to practice what they preach. We must come together and reunite and reignite a fire that will be so Holy Spirit authentic that it will draw the lost, the strayed, the struggling, the straight, and the crooked back to real life-changing Church where Christ is exalted sincerely and entirely. We must move away from fan-based ideology and ministry and begin to make real followers of Jesus Christ.

I am aware that many churches are doing a lot of good and integral endeavors, but we cannot overlook the great fall away from the Church Body. We have been conforming to cultures as oppose to transforming cultures to walk in the ways of Christ. We have great networking programs, conferences, and conventions, but how has these expensive "let's just have more church" events increased the spiritual net worth of those who are in attendance. We have allowed some of these mediums to become platforms that launch the careers of men and women, and we've done it on the back of financially struggling people who give maximum output, but get minimum in return. No follow up, no follow through, only an invitation for registration to come back the next year.

I know that some of these words and criticisms may appear to be an attack on certain groups, but trust me. It's not. I was once a part of the problem, even though my intentions were good as I'm sure others have had good intentions also. But good intentions are not always God intentions, and if you know you were and may still be a part of the problem, then why not consider being a part of the solution. Our voices must become more amplified toward other issues that people are confronted with in their daily lives. We must use our voices, not in just an audible sense, but in an action sense. We cannot continue to be distracted by things that are designed to take us away from the real issues that plague our world: the poverty rates, the Black male incarceration rates, the unemployment rates, the drug addiction rates, the abortion rates, the murder and crime rates, the illiteracy rates, and the fatherless children rates. We are called to be voices and vehicles that take authority over these vices that have left our communities and citizens vulnerable to life-depressing situations.

I do not have all of the answers, but I'm willing to be a part of a real conversation that is more than just television camera hype. I have attempted to unmask a problem within the Body of Christ, and I tried to be a creditable voice, and not just a cynical critic who wants arguments and no answers. The rich shepherd poor sheep idea was to expose an identity that is poisonous to the Body of Christ. We must love the sheep as Jesus loves them and invest in their prosperity as much as we use them to invest in ours. Remember, rich shepherds should be birthing rich sheep. I hope that everything good will come out of this, all to the Glory of God. It is my prayer that the issues at hand and the instructions given will become an educational discipline for future generations to follow. We must not continue to reproduce situations that are a detriment and robbery to God's innocent little lambs. May we get back to the real message of the Gospel and abandon all false teachings that do not line up with the Word of God. Thank you for reading this book, and I pray that you have been richly blessed, edified, and convicted. Pay close attention to the next page. If you feel as though you are in need of help as a senior pastor, read the information, contact us, and let our team help you to get back on the path to total restoration. God bless you and keep you!

Carlos L. Malone, Sr.

CONTACT THE AUTHOR
GRACE RESTORATION NETWORK

"THE PERFECT NETWORK FOR IMPERFECT PEOPLE"

Biblical Foundation:

Brethren if a man be overtaken in a fault, ye which are spiritual, restore such an one in the spirit of meekness; considering thyself, lest thou also be tempted. Galatians 6:1

Vision:

To be a conduit of compassion that exemplifies grace, mercy, and love to those who are struggling with or have succumbed to their sin.

Mission:

To create an environment within Christendom that is free from religious criticism and self-righteous judgments. We are aiming to be the network where Christian leaders who struggle in their flesh can find substantive nurturing, support, and healing for their sin struggling failures.

Core Value:

To remain trustworthy, transparent, and true to those whom we are graciously allowed to serve.

GRN is a ministry leaders support network for those persons in senior ministry leadership positions who have been overtaken by the struggles of an uncontrollable flesh and desire to sin. Level of position leaves no person exempt from a potential failure or fall. Note that the vulnerability is oftentimes greater when you serve in high-level positions of responsibility. The intentional purpose of our network is to protect the character net-worth of those who are a part of our network family. We are well aware that the vessels that carry these valuable gifts are carrying them based on the value of the giver Himself and the gift itself, but never the gifted themselves.

> "For we preach not ourselves, but Christ Jesus the Lord; and ourselves your servants for Jesus' sake. For God, who commanded the light to shine out of darkness, hath shined in our hearts, to give the light of the knowledge of the glory of God in the face of Jesus Christ. But we have this treasure in earthen vessels, that the Excellency of the power may be of God, and not of us."
> — 2 Corinthians 4:5–7, KJV

With these truths in mind, it becomes our strategy to be proactive, precautionary, and prepared before a crisis, so when they happen—and they will happen—we'll have a system in place to effectively manage the impending crisis. Oftentimes, in many religious reformations, there are unbiblical disciplines that are crowd pleasing disciplines that are laced with a pharisaic ideology that only knows how to put people out when they fall, but never pull them up when they do. We must always remember that the person who fell into sin is the same person whom God was using prior to his or her sin. And God, who is omniscient, knew in advance that these events would occur, but yet He called them and assigned them. We must never allow the sins that man commits to become the defining conclusions of who they are. Many times, the things we do are not an indication of who we are. But, unfortunately, that's the power and complexity of the human struggle. *"Stumbling doesn't have to mean Crumbling."*

The information presented here is just a very brief synopsis of what the GNR is undertaking to help struggling leaders. If you need more information, please visit carlosmalone.com. We will be officially launching this support group network in the Spring of 2019.

Join The Grace Restoration Network and help us bring true healing to the Body of Christ throughout the world. Email us at:

gracerestorationnetwork@gmail.com.

About the Author

Carlos L. Malone, Sr. is an apostle, prophet, pastor, teacher, entrepreneur, motivational speaker and author. His style of teaching is refreshing, authentic and genuine. His bold approach to deliverance and spiritual wholeness through transparency is a biblical blueprint for those seeking a better way of life in God for their families, professions, communities, wealth and health. The five-fold ministry anointing upon his life continues equip and impact ministries throughout the United States and abroad.

He began preaching and teaching as a youth on April 21, 1977 in East St. Louis, Illinois, transitioning, building and edifying the body of Christ with indisputable kingdom principles, which he still employs to this day.

Apostle Malone has served as the servant leader of The Bethel Church, Miami Florida for 29 years. TBC is a ministry that embraces all of the gifts God has given to the body of Christ for the purpose of its maturation and effectiveness. He has witnessed incredible growth and the transformation of a church that has become a trailblazing entity that has nurtured many churches and pastors around the world. Under his apostolic leadership, more than 150 men and women have been licensed and ordained as elders, prophets, evangelist, pastors, teachers and ministers. Several of whom have launched churches and continue to enhance the Body of Christ.

Apostle Malone is the Founder/CEO of Rhema Apostolic International Network (R.A.I.N.), an apostolic training network for those who desire to walk in spiritual authority and wholeness through training, transformation and triumphing through God's kingdom agenda. He is also launching in the Spring of 2019, Grace Restoration Network (GRN), "the perfect network for imperfect people. This network is designed to be a support ministry network whose sole purpose is for the restoration and healing of leaders who fall into unfortunate trappings that impact the integrity of their character. He believes there is a hunger in the land for something meatier and less sweet, more substantive and less shallow, more spiritual and less spirited, more transparent and less pretentious. There is a rumbling in the heavens; it's time for God's people to be set free from religion layered spirituality.

Apostle Malone has written several books which include The Rib Connection, The Integrity of Ministry, God's Created Order, Hidden in His Hands, The Prevailing Prayer Life, The Road to Purpose-The Journey Beyond Potential, The Reward of Purging, and ME; Your Life Transformation and Empowerment Guide.

Apostle Malone's creative talents are extensive. He has shared his gift of song and worship for more than five decades. Known world-wide for his tenor voice on such recordings as; "Bethel in Praise," "Thirst No More," and "A New Thing" also featuring Bishop Paul S. Morton, Kirk Franklin, Be-Be Winans, Byron Cage, the late Daryl Coley and a host of other artists. He has produced and directed theatrical works including "Jesus for the People" and "O' Come Let Us Adore Him, "The Beginning," and "The Beginning Again," an artistic presentation of the creation narratives.

He is a devoted husband to his lovely wife Pamela; a loving father to his children — twin daughters Ashley and Andrea, son Carlos, Jr. and his beloved godson Raymond Young. A new addition to his family is Derby Bernadel, the husband of Andrea whom he refers to as his son, not son-in-law. All of this is what gives historical reference and significance to the life of Apostle Carlos L. Malone, Sr.